Yesterday's Detroit

Seemann's Historic Cities Series

Seemann's Historic Cities Series No. 9

Yesterday's
DETROIT

by Frank Angelo

E. A. Seemann Publishing, Inc.
Miami, Florida

Many individuals and institutions kindly supported the author's task in collecting photographs. Their contributions are gratefully acknowledged (in abbreviated form) at the end of each caption:

Board of Ed.	Detroit Board of Education.
Burton	Burton Historical Collection, Detroit Public Library.
Buyse	Leon Buyse, historian for Detroit's Belgian community.
Chrysler	Chrysler Motors Archives.
DHM	Detroit Historical Museum.
DIA	Detroit Institute of Arts.
Detroit	City of Detroit, Reports and Information Committee.
Clements	William L. Clements Library, University of Michigan.
Det. Bank	Detroit Bank & Trust.
Ford	Ford Archives.
Free Press	The Detroit Free Press.
GM	General Motors.
HPL	Hamtramck Public Library.
Int. Institute	International Institute of Detroit
Jellinek	Mrs. Edna Jellinek, of Detroit.
Katz	Irving I. Katz, executive secretary, Temple Beth El.
Keane	Leontine Keane, Wayne State University.
Keydel	Kurt Keydel, publisher, *The Abend-Post*.
Kushner	Aid Kushner, former Detroit Lions trainer.
Lions	The Detroit Lions, public relations department.
London	Milton H. London, Metropolitan Exhibitors Inc.
Luttermoser	The Edward Luttermoser family.
McMullan	Mrs. Ralph A. McMullan, Scandinavian Orchestra
MDCV	Metropolitan Detroit Convention and Visitors Bureau
MVMA	Motor Vehicle Manufacturers Association.
Mich. Bell	Michigan Bell Telephone Company.
Mich. Con.	Michigan Consolidated Gas Company, Public Information Department.
Musicians Union	Detroit Federation of Musicians.
News	The Detroit News.
Red Cross	Detroit chapter, American Red Cross.
Rypsam	Mrs. Alyce Rypsam, of Detroit.
Scarab	Scarab Club
UCS	United Community Services, public affairs department.
U. of D.	University of Detroit, community affairs department.
Wayne	Wayne State University, Archives of Labor History and Urban Affairs.
Wehmeier	Victor Wehmeier, Detroit Boat Club historian.
Woodard	Clarence C. Woodard, Detroit Fire Department historian.

```
Library of Congress Cataloging in Publication Data

Angelo, Frank.
   Yesterday's Detroit.

   (Seemann's historic cities series, no. 9)
   1.  Detroit--Description--Views.  2.  Detroit--
History--Pictorial works.  I.  Title.
F574.D4A68        917.74'34'030222        74-75292
ISBN 0-912458-37-2
```

Manufactured in the United States of America

Contents

Preface

WRITING A BOOK about one's hometown can be a heartwarming experience—and heartbreaking, too.

It's heartwarming because one is forced to look deeply into a history that, it turns out, had been only dimly perceived. Now, the need for the precision of facts and perspective demanded of an author leads to books, archives, piles of pictures, and many other sources which few people realize are available.

It's heartbreaking because, despite this wealth of material, the limitation of space forces one barely to scratch the surface, and there is the realization of omissions that are troublesome to accept.

But then, there is some consolation. This is a first book and it does, in good measure, approach the modest goal that was set for it—to present, at a time when so many are looking back, some visual reminders of what Detroit was before the Korean War when it and the rest of the country plunged into new horizons.

Two things became evident rather quickly in putting together this book. I couldn't escape the perceptions of Detroit that I have accumulated over a period of almost 60 years, so there inevitably is a personal perspective in the presentation. And secondly, it could never have been done without an unusual amount of cooperation from scores of people.

To name them all is impossible, but it is important to name a few whose assistance was particularly critical.

First there was Lee Hills, who triggered the whole idea as he has done so many good things for me over the years.

Then there were those who made available the pictures. Credits appear on another page and are keyed to individual pictures, but mention should be made of especially extensive efforts and contributions of the Detroit Free Press library staff and Chief Photographer Tony Spina, of Dr. Phil Mason and Mrs. Margery Long at Wayne State; Mrs. Alice Dalligan and the Burton Historical Collection staff; Solan Weeks and the Detroit Historical Museum staff; Henry Edmonds and Winthrop Sears, Jr., who dug deep and often into the Ford Archives, and Mrs. Bea Adamski, of the Hamtramck Public Library.

There are scores of others who contributed or put up with all sorts of requests and irritations. They know that I treasure the memory of what they did and I trust they, including Betty, Frank Junior, and Andrew whose views are particularly meaningful to me, will be pleased with the result.

FRANK ANGELO

Detroit
May, 1974

DETROIT WAS STRUGGLING to survive about the time surveys were being taken for this map by Joseph de Lerys. Appeals from the French commandant brought several hundred French settlers from Canada and in 1755 another influx came when many Acadians banished from Nova Scotia found refuge here. In 1760, when it was surrendered to the British, the fort had an area of 372 feet by 600 feet, about 300 dwellings and a population of 2,000. (Clements)

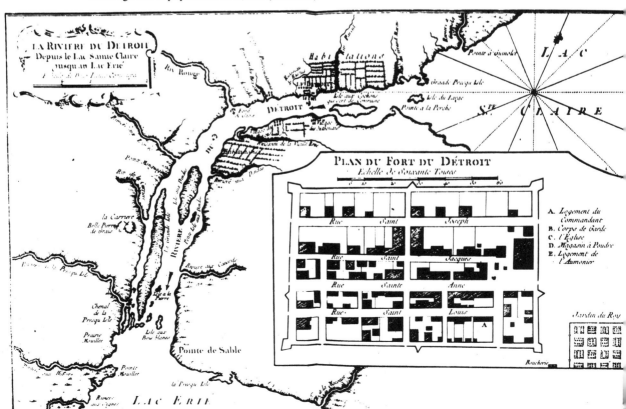

The First 189 Years

FIRST IT WAS Antoine Laumet de la Mothe Cadillac who dreamt of the potential of the land that eventually would be called Detroit—and thousands have come after him to give of their hearts, their minds, and their muscle in building the fifth largest city in America.

Cadillac was a soldier, an adventurer, a man who dreamt of prosperity for himself and greatness in the New World for France, his homeland.

He planted a seed but it was left to those who came later to create a community that would provide opportunity for the individual and open great vistas for social and economic progress to society everywhere.

Cadillac first saw the lake country when he became commandant of Fort Michilimackinac in northern Michigan in 1694. It was there that he heard of "the deep, clear river," of the straits ("Le Detroit"), of an area that was as "richly set with islands as is a queen's necklace with jewels", and thought of how it could be "the center of the lake country, the gateway to the west."

So he convinced his King, Louis XIV, and Count Pontchartrain, France's minister of marine at the time, to give him the opportunity to go there. He was provided with 1,500 livres (about $300) to build a fort, 15 arpents square (225 acres) to put it on, and a subsistence allowance for his wife and two children (he and Therese were to have 13 eventually).

On June 2, 1701, he left Montreal with about 100 men and 25 canoes and, after he reached Georgian Bay, he headed for the west coast of Lake Huron. Finally, late on the afternoon of July 23, he passed the spot where he would build his fort and camped overnight on Grosse Ile. The next day, within hours of his decision to build his fort, on the high, north bank of the river, the first trees were felled and, symbolically, the first building completed was St. Anne's church, a 24½-by-35 foot edifice with a 10-foot beam.

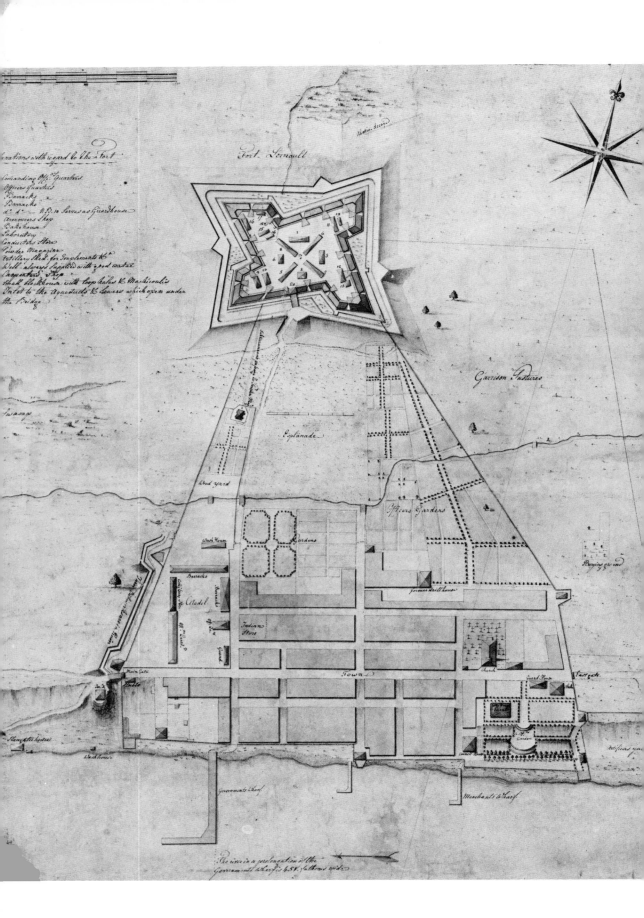

Opposite page: FIRST MAJOR EXPANSION at Detroit came with the building of Fort Lernoult, starting in 1778. Capt. Richard Beringer Lernoult, commandant, was concerned about defending against American attacks. A covered passageway connected it to the old stockade. Work ceased in 1784 with the end of the Revolutionary War. Fort Lernoult covered roughly an area bounded by Lafayette and Congress, between Griswold and Washington Boulevard. (Clements)

Right: MAJOR HENRY GLADWIN'S tenacity proved to be a decisive factor in Detroit's early history. He arrived in September, 1761, shortly after the British had taken over. He found himself with a garrison of about 100 men inside a palisade of 12- to 15-foot high log pickets to face the challenge of Chief Pontiac. He did. This portrait, by John Hall, an English painter of the 18th Century, is in the Detroit Institute of Arts. (DIA)

It was tough work. Wrote Cadillac:

"All of this is no easy task, as everything has to be carried on the shoulders, for we have no oxen or horses yet to draw loads, nor to plough, and to accomplish it, it is necessary to be very active."

Primitive as things were, and would remain for many years (the first street light using gas was installed 150 years later) some roots were laid for the future. The first wheat was planted that fall and harvested in July, 1702. Cadillac's wife and Madame de Tonty, the wife of his Assistant Lieutenant Tonty, arrived in mid-1702, and by 1708, 63 inhabitants had lots inside the fort, and 29 farms were worked outside.

It took some time for Cadillac to establish his control because there were others bidding for the lucrative trade in furs, especially beaver, which was at the heart of the commercial development and which remained a factor in Detroit well into the 1800s.

Those who wanted to do business in Detroit after 1706 had to pay Cadillac, and there were some who objected. A certain M. Joseph Parent, for instance, was upset because the privilege of shoeing horses cost him 600 francs, two hogsheads of ale, and the shoeing of all of Cadillac's horses.

St. Anne's still survives, not too far actually from its original site, and the names of those who were among the first to get grants of land for strip farms that ran to the river on the east side also are part of the city's heritage in family and street names—Campau, Beaubien, Chene, and Dequindre being among them.

Before Cadillac left in 1711 to become the governor of Louisiana, he also had achieved friendly relations with several Indian tribes, and more than 2,-000 Indians lived within sight of the fort. But it wasn't until the late 1740s that the French made any major effort to build up the settlement, and this was to be short-lived.

The British had started their campaign to expand their hold in the New

World. In 1760, after the fall of Montreal to General Wolfe, Fort Pontchartrain was surrendered by the French with all of Canada.

A British captain wrote that "the inhabitants seem very happy at the change in government, but they are in great want of everything. The fort is much better than expected."

Detroit's population was 2,000 and there were about 300 buildings inside the fort which covered the area now bounded roughly by Griswold on the east, Washington Boulevard on the west, Larned on the north, and the river on the south.

With the coming of the British on November 16, 1760, Detroit's role as a commercial center expanded, and a whole new approach to the Indians developed. The French had counted heavily on them to aid in their efforts at colonization; the British saw no need for such close relationships. And there came a dramatic moment when the British proved their point—and barely saved Detroit.

It happened on the morning of May 8, 1763, when Major Henry Gladwin, the commandant of British forces at the time, reached over to pull aside one Indian's blanket, revealing a sawed-off rifle. Thus, the conspiracy of Chief Pontiac was broken.

"Pontiac was a man of extraordinary will-power and possessed of compelling personality," wrote historian Goerge Catlin. So it was no fool who plotted the elimination of whites from this area. His idea was to bring together various tribes to stage simultaneous attacks on forts throughout a 200,000 square-mile area.

Plans were laid at a grand council in April for action in early May. Pontiac himself was to lead a group of sixty chiefs in the attack on Detroit.

There are several versions of how the plot developed and of how General Gladwin learned of it, but learn of it he did. One version is that on the morning of May 8 when Pontiac approached, he noted that British soldiers were everywhere, and on the alert. Still, he moved slowly through the village to his rendezvous with Gladwin.

As the story goes, Pontiac asked: "Why does my English brother keep his young men armed and on parade as if ready for battle? Does he expect the French?"

Gladwin answered that by practicing his men were kept ready to fight well if war should come. Pontiac then launched into a speech in which he talked of eternal friendship and goodwill. As a token of his sincerity, he offered Gladwin a belt of wampum.

Pontiac reached for the wampum. By pre-arranged signal, Gladwin's of-

WAMPUM, once used as money by the Indians in this area, is white, purple or black beads made from shells. It was made into belts or was woven into clothing, often strung on a strip of animal skin. (Det. Bank)

12

CONSIDERED THE FIRST authentic view of Detroit is this wash drawing of 1794 *(above)* by an unknown artist. Years later much of the area in which ships are shown anchored was filled in. Other early views included one of St. Anne's Street *(right),* and one from the Canadian side done in 1804 by Edward Walsh, a British doctor *(below).* (Burton-Clements)

SOLID PROGRESS began in 1813 when General Lewis Cass assumed the governorship of the Territory of Michigan. By the time he departed to become Secretary of War in 1831, the foundation had been laid for the future growth of both Detroit and the state. He had a distinguished career as U.S. senator, candidate for the presidency, and Secretary of State just before the Civil War. He died in Detroit in 1866 at age 84. His wife is shown at left. (Free Press)

DETROIT began its surge from this small area. This drawing portrays, in correct detail, the city of 1818.
(Free Press)

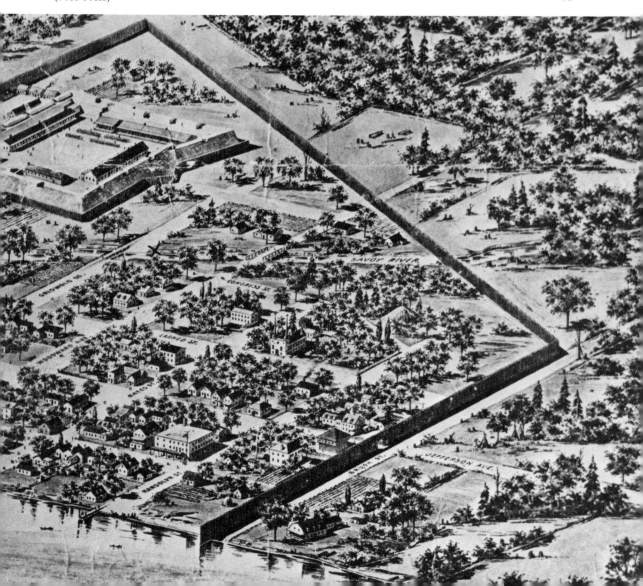

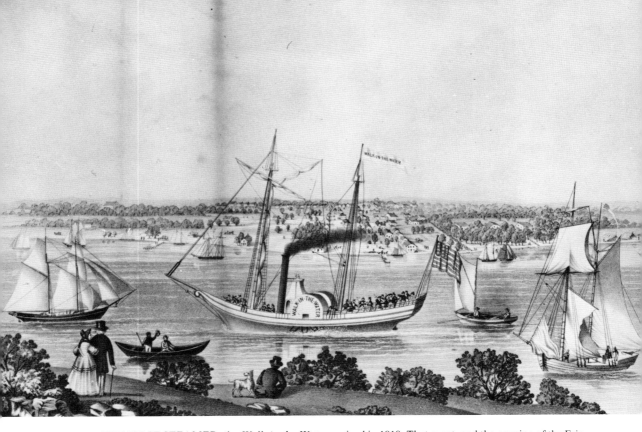

THE FIRST STEAMER, the *Walk-in-the-Water,* arrived in 1818. That event, and the opening of the Erie Canal, enabled thousands to come from the East and from foreign countries. By 1837, steamers were literally jamming the harbor, and arrivals numbered hundreds of people daily. (Clements-DIA)

ficers drew their swords and drums in the barrack's room rolled. It was then that Gladwin stepped to one of the Indians, pulled aside his blanket and revealed the shortened gun.

In the days that followed, there was bloodshed and suffering and it wasn't until 153 days later that a siege imposed by Pontiac ended. Eventually, on July 23, 1766, Pontiac signed a treaty of peace, proclaiming his allegiance to the British.

Detroit remained basically a fort and trading post into the 1800s, but the period saw more than a few changes of "the people in charge." The British continued in control for more than 30 years after the Pontiac siege. Some expansion took place with the addition of Fort Lernoult in 1778, just north of the original fort, but at the time the American flag went up at noon of July 11, 1796, Detroit's population was 2,200, and it dropped sharply as many British left for Canada.

Adjustment came slowly. On January 18, 1802, Detroit was incorporated as a town under a charter of the Northwest Territory's legislature, and the first election was held in May. Taxes to cover a budget of $150 were assessed on the basis of 25 cents on each individual 21 and over, plus a quarter of one percent on homes.

But then came another of those shocking moments that seem to mark the history of Detroit.

On June 11,1805, a fire started in the barn of one John Harvey, the village baker, destroying all but one of the town's 300 buildings.

It was a windy day. Harvey planned to drive to the local mill to replenish his flour supply. He hitched his horse to the two-wheel cart that was, and would remain for some time, the mode of transportation for Detroiters. Sparks from his pipe bothered him, and when he banged the pipe against his boot in the way of one trying to extinguish it, the fiery plug fell out and was blown into a pile of hay.

Hours later, after valiant efforts with axes, battering rams, and a bucket brigade to bring water directly from the river, all that was left standing was an old warehouse and several stone chimneys.

Father Gabriel Richard was among those stunned by the catastrophe, but not for long. In a short time he was mustering the French farmers along the river, and soon they were helping to provide food, shelter, and solace.

There was something eery about the timing of the fire because only hours after it had subsided, there appeared on the scene the first members of the Governors and Judges' group, newly constituted by Federal officials to govern the Territory of Michigan.

Among them was Governor William Hull and Judge Augustus B. Woodward who was to leave an everlasting imprint on the city. To begin with, they assumed almost dictatorial control. In fact, it was 1824, when a new charter went into effect and John R. Williams was elected first mayor, before civil government once more was totally in the hands of Detroiters.

The instinct of the people who had been burned out was to begin rebuilding immediately on the sites of their old homes, but Woodward particularly urged patience. It was he who came up with a plan to serve as the basis on which the Detroit of the future would expand.

Woodward's plan featured streets ranging from 200 feet to 60 feet in width, plus squares (Campus Martius), circular parks (Grand Circus Park), and triangular ones (what is now Capitol Park.) Some said he had the Washington, D.C., design in mind when he did it.

There was controversy to be sure, but finally Woodward and Hull went to Washington for approval. They got it by an Act of Congress on April 21, 1806. The act provided for establishing a Land Board to lay out the town on the old site, plus an additional 10,000 acres.

"Every person above the age of seventeen years who owned or inhabited a house in Detroit at the time of the fire, and who does not profess or owe allegiance to a foreign power" was to get a lot.

It may be instructive in the 1970s to note that, according to Silas Farmer, lobbying and how it was done had some familiar overtones.

"It would appear that members of Congress even then," Farmer writes, "were credited with being open to the influences of conviviality, for Judge Woodward is quoted as saying that he expended $300 in wine to treat the members of Congress with the purpose of influencing them to pass the bill."

Then Farmer adds another note with a familiar ring:

"All the old records show that there was gross mismanagement and vexatious delays in the distribution of the lots."

Woodward remained a central figure in Detroit's story for years, but for all his efforts in helping to establish the first university in Michigan, for all his contributions to city planning, for all his administration of justice, he apparently was, in the full sense of the word, a "character." Farmer calls him "an eccentric genius" who had "peculiarities of manner so marked and slovenliness so extreme as to almost defy description."

One example: During a thundershower he might sit in a chair outside his door to take his shower.

Woodward was a Virginian, a tall, sallow-faced bachelor who enjoyed his libations. He is reported to have kept a glass of brandy at his side while on the bench, in addition to making it a point each evening to smoke his pipe and chat and sip whiskey until he had had his regular half-pint.

Interestingly, Farmer seems apologetic in calling attention to all this but, Farmer said, he did it because Woodward's acts are not above reproach.

One of the more questionable aspects of Woodward's activities came dur-

FATHER GABRIEL RICHARD (*above* and *right*) provided much for the early spiritual, educational and cultural life of the city. He arrived in June, 1798, and became the pastor of Saint Anne's in 1802. In the years that followed he published Detroit's first newspaper, the *Michigan Essay or, The Impartial Observer,* in 1809; started four schools, two for girls and two for boys; brought the first organ to Detroit; and was elected to Congress as a representative of the Territory of Michigan in 1823. He died while ministering to the ill during a cholera epidemic in 1832. (Free Press)

MICHIGAN ESSAY,

OR, THE IMPARTIAL OBSERVER.

DETROIT, TERRITORY OF MICHIGAN:—PRINTED AND PUBLISHED BY JAMES M. MILLER.

VOL. I.]   THURSDAY, AUGUST 31, 1809.   [NO.

TERMS
OF THE MICHIGAN ESSAY.

IT will be published every Thursday; and handed to City subscribers, at 5 dollars per ann payable half-yearly, in advance. Other Subscribers, resident in

were advancing. In th. Turkish memca, .e hav. g failed to super Croatia, the Turks had risen in ced Mr. Erskine, who so far ex arms, and had invaded the Austri ceeded his powers of instruction, an part of that country. They that the British government will had taken Celtin and Dresnick: not satify the stipulations he had and had already possession of a entered into with the U. States.— considerable part of that country. Mr. Erskine is, of course, recalled By letters from Triest-, the and the general opinion here is, French flag was displayed in that we shall u questionably have war place on the 28th May. The with America. Tar, which sold a

From the Commonwealth.

SALT WORKS.

Much advantage is expected to tha ublic, from the great and valuable im rovements making near the town of But ler. In particular the salt works com menced by THOMAS COLLINS, Esq. de serve public encouragemen. The spring of saline water, is about a mile and a ha N. E of Butler, and only thirty miles

PROTESTANT CHURCHES began to appear in Detroit in the 1820s, and by the 1840s the East Side of Woodward Avenue, between Congress and Larned, included several of them. In this drawing from the Silas Farmer book, from left to right, are the First Methodist Episcopal Church, the Old Burchard Building, Saint Paul's Episcopal Church, the session room, and then the First Presbyterian Church. In 1850 there were 18 churches in Detroit, including two for the black population. Temple Beth El, the first Jewish congregation, was organized on September 22, 1850, by 12 German Jews meeting at the home of Isaac and Sarah Cozens. (Burton)

TWO SISTERS provided money in their wills to build the Mariners' Church which has become one of Detroit's most revered landmarks. It was built of stone, and the first floor originally was designed for business purposes. The post office was one of the first tenants. The church was consecrated on December 23, 1849. More than 100 years later it was moved intact from its original site as part of the city's riverfront redevelopment. (Burton)

DEPTH OF FEELING among Catholics in Detroit is suggested by this welcoming arch built when Father John Samuel Foley arrived to become Bishop of Detroit in November, 1888. You're looking north on Washington Boulevard from the corner of Michigan. (News)

ing the period of August 6, 1812, to September 28, 1813, when the British once again occupied Detroit during the war of 1812.

Governor Hull shocked the country by surrendering the city and 2,000 men, 40 barrels of powder, 400 rounds of 24-pound shot, and large supplies of provisions to the British, but Woodward stayed on as justice during the occupation.

However, because he apparently did fight for some of the rights of the citizenry against the military governor, Woodward's action was excused. He remained active in the city's affairs until his retirement in 1823.

In the years after the War of 1812 (Detroit's population at that moment was about 850) the town began slowly to emerge from its status as a trading and military outpost (the stockade was removed and the fort demolished in 1827).

DETROIT'S FIRST GASLIGHTS appeared in 1851, just about the time the city was beginning to establish the foundation for its industrial development. In the decade before the Civil War, Detroit began the building of railroad cars, stoves, and ships, and it also had plants producing matches, tobacco products, iron, drugs, and paints. The dome of the Michigan Central Railroad roundhouse *(above)* located on Woodbridge between Fifth and Sixth, dominated the area which also included the gasworks. Spectators got a great view of the city from the top of the "wheat depot", which preceded erection of the first grain elevator for that railway. A typical gaslight is shown in the street scene at left in the early 1880s. (DHM-Mich. Con.)

New men came on the scene, led by Lewis Cass, who was named Governor of the Territory and would serve until 1831. There was the beginning of schools and newspapers and in 1817 of a state university which Woodward called the Catholepistemaid or the University of Michigania. The Rev. John Monteith, who dedicated the first Protestant church on February 27, 1820, and Father Richard were named president and vice president, and held all 13 professorships.

Newcomers were mostly from the New England states and their numbers grew as the coming of the lake steamers and the opening of the Erie Canal in 1825 cut traveling time from Detroit to the East from months to days.

Something of a morale booster was the first visit by a United States president in 1817. When citizens learned that James Monroe was coming, they planned a procession through the streets and a fireworks display. The night of his arrival, August 13, the city was specially illuminated at a cost of $23.26, as were vessels in the harbor. Monroe stayed five days, and Detroiters gave him a brace of horses and a carriage as a gift.

The *Walk-in-the-Water*, built in Buffalo, was the historic steamer that broke the transportation barrier, and the people of Detroit were there to take note. The *Detroit Gazette* of August 28, 1818, provided the following report:

"Yesterday, between the hours of 10 and 11 A.M., the elegant steamboat Walk-in-the-Water, Captain J. Fisk, arrived. As she passed the public wharf that's owned by Mr. J. S. Roby, she was cheered by hundreds of the inhabitants who had collected to witness this (in their waters) truly novel and grand spectacle. She came to Wing's Wharf.

"She left Buffalo at half past one on the 23rd . . . the whole time employed in sailing (not including several stops en route) in this first voyage from Buffalo to this port, being about 44 hours and 10 minutes, the wind ahead during nearly the whole voyage."

Walk-in-the-Water made the trip to Buffalo once in two weeks, carrying up to 100 passengers at $18 for a cabin, but by 1837 Detroit handled as many as 37 steamers a day.

It was 1822 before Detroit had its first stagecoach service and 1831 before the first railroad, the Pontiac and Detroit, was even chartered. Another historic moment drew a large crowd on August 21, 1830, when the first substantial waterworks went into operation. As the water began flowing through three-inch pipes, Governor Cass was moved to exclaim: "Fellow citizens, what an age of progress!"

And indeed it proved to be, although there were moments in 1832, 1834, 1849, and 1854, when the ravages of cholera caused concern. The 1834 attack was particularly severe, with almost seven percent of the population dying in a month.

Out of it, however, came the dramatic story of the Rev. Martin Kundig, who converted Holy Trinity Church, which had just been established, into a hospital. Holy Trinity served the Irish community, just as St. Anne's was for the French. In later years, other Catholic churches came into being to serve the needs of new groups as they arrived.

In 1830, Detroit's population was 2,222, and then came a land boom in the Territory that went bust about the time that Michigan was granted statehood in 1837. Detroit was the capital and remained so until 1847 when the state government moved to Lansing. But Detroit was also what Cadillac had foreseen: the gateway not only to expansion in Michigan but for areas to the west.

From the very start of its nineteenth-century growth Detroit attracted a diversity of people in sizeable numbers. The Germans in 1825 and the Irish in the 1830s came in the first major migration. By 1870, almost half of the population of 79,577 was foreign born. In 1880, the census additionally showed more than 40 nationalities represented, ranging from a total of 17,292 Germans to one single Greek.

FIRST TO GO off to war in 1861 was the 780-man strong First Michigan Volunteer Infantry which was presented with the colors on May 13 in this Campus Martius ceremony. The Andrews Rail Road Hotel is on the site later taken by the Detroit Opera House. The spire of the First Protestant Church, at what is now the site of the downtown library, can also be seen. The First Michigan led the advance in the capture of Alexandria, Va., and suffered heavy losses at Bull Run. (Burton)

A FRONTIER-TOWN ATMOSPHERE prevailed in Detroit in 1860 when people gathered in Campus Martius, at Woodward and Michigan. Detroit's population was 45,619 and it ranked 19th among American cities. Years later the Majestic and then the 21-story First Federal Building would be on this corner. (Burton)

The Irish gravitated to the area between Fifth and Sixth streets which became known as Corktown, and the area for several blocks along Gratiot Avenue on the east side was often referred to as Dutchtown or the German quarter.

By mid-century, Detroit had become the 21st largest city in America and had exhibited many of the characteristics that were to stay with it in the years ahead.

A system of plank roads leading out of Detroit was established. They followed precisely the paths of today's main arteries—Michigan, Grand River, Woodward, Gratiot, and Jefferson. There were fine residential areas on its approximately ninety streets, and the first signs of major industry emerged as the value of Michigan's timber, iron ore, copper, and other natural resources became apparent.

Gaslights began to replace in 1851 the use of tallow candles or lamps which burned lard and whale oil, but the curfew bell rang at six in the morning, noon, and six and nine at night, to give the citizens the time.

Politics were tough, as suggested by an ad appearing just before an election in 1838:

"To the Poor—The Whigs will distribute one hundred dollars in bread and

WEST SIDE of Woodward Avenue between Congress and Fort Street in the early 1870s. The new City Hall can be seen just beyond the McMillan Grocery. (Burton)

pork among the city poor tomorrow evening . . . Time and place will be given in the morning paper.''

But a wave of morality swept the city. In 1841, for example, one item of business before the council was adoption of a resolution that provided for demolition of a house of prostitution. All other means to close it had failed. The house was leveled on November 16, and the city was sued. In 1857 there were reports of people setting fires to similar places, all of which points up the fact that it wasn't until 1865 that the city, reluctantly, established a fulltime, paid police department.

But as the economic, social, and spiritual life of the community began to take shape (for example, the first Jewish synagogue, Temple Beth El, was founded in 1850), there came the Civil War. Detroit was no stranger to slavery (there were 78 male and 101 female slaves in the city in 1782), and it knew the trauma of racism and toil of trying to do something about it.

The city was jolted by an incident in 1833 when blacks of that time used force to help Thornton Blackburn and his wife escape to Canada after they had been arrested as fugitive slaves. Mobs also ravaged and burned the homes of black people in 1863 when William Faulkner was arrested, tried, and convicted of raping a white girl. He was later shown to have been innocent. In each case, troops were called out to help keep the peace.

But there were brighter spots. In 1837, an Anti-Slavery Society was organized, and for many years Detroit also was the focal point for the "Underground Railroad" by which slaves were moved from one place to another from all parts of the country to freedom in Canada.

26

STREETCARS of the horse-drawn variety *(right)* made their first appearance in
1863 on Jefferson Avenue, and the first
electric streetcar ran out Woodward in
1893. In 1922, after an extended and often
bitter fight, the question of municipal
ownership was settled and the Department of Street Railways (DSR) took over.
On April 7, 1956, the system phased out
the last streetcar and switched completely
to buses. Horse-drawn cars went as far
north as a spot near the present viaduct,
just south of Milwaukee, before turning
back. Above is scene on Woodward
Avenue near Jefferson in horse-drawn era
and the same spot *(below)* in the early
1900s with streetcars and an interurban
(center rails) sharing the stage with horse-
drawn carts. (DHM-Burton)

MOMENTS BEFORE UNVEILING of the Soldiers and Sailors monument on Campus Martius on April 9, 1872. The idea was first broached just after the start of the Civil War and revived in 1865. Funds came from school children, the Masonic, Odd Fellows, and Good Templar organizations and ladies' auxiliaries. The design was done by Randolph Rogers, a former Ann Arborite who was living in Rome at the time. The monument cost $70,000, stands 60 feet tall, and has remained a basic landmark while the heart of the city has changed. (Wayne)

And in the Civil War itself, Detroit and Michigan played a major role. Within hours after the first shot was fired at Fort Sumter on April 12, 1861, an infantry regiment fully armed, clothed, and equipped was mobilized. It arrived in Washington May 16, the first western regiment there. A bit ironically, the First Michigan Colored Infantry was mustered into service and left Detroit just a few days after the Faulkner riot.

Michigan sent 90,747 men to war (6,000 of them from Detroit) of whom 14,343 died of various causes. On November 8, 1870, the citizens of Michigan voted to eliminate the word "white" from their constitution, and the first blacks cast their votes.

With the end of the Civil War, there came the beginning of new migrations and expansions of business and industry which had begun to grow in the 1840s and 1850s. The population almost quadrupled from 45,619 to 205,876 between 1860 and 1890, and with it so did the value of goods produced and sold.

Detroit presented an interesting diversity in its manufacturing, ranging from tobacco to shoes to steel to seeds, to stoves to railroad cars to drugs and assorted other products.

The great company names were Michigan Car Company, Detroit Car Wheel Company, D. M. Ferry Seed, Detroit Stove Company, Parke-Davis, Frederick Stearns Pharmaceutical Mfg. Co., The American Eagle Tobacco Company, Pingree-Smith Shoe Factory, etc.

And the men who made these companies and others move included Eber B. Ward, James McMillan, Zachariah Chandler, John J. Bagley, George B. Russel, Richard H. Fyfe, James Vernor, Hazen Pingree, George Hammond, to name only a few.

Business moved north up to Jefferson Avenue starting in the 1830s, but it wasn't until 1860 that there was much development on Woodward north of Jefferson and not until 1870 before it swept past Campus Martius. It was about that time that C. R. Mabley opened the first department store.

Much of the business of the day was done on a person-to-person basis. As Farmer described it:

"One hears the ting-a-ling-ting-ting-ting of the scissors grinder, who presently appears with wheels and treadle on his back; the toot of the ragman's horn, and the calls of 'Glass put in,' 'Umbrellas to mend—to mend.' And the newsboy's cry is heard omnipresent as are the vigorous and clear "Tatoes, Fresh Fruit, Strawberries' of the vegetable man."

So as Detroit moved closer to the era of the automobile which was to bring on a new and even more astonishing flood of people and ideas, the character of the city had been formed.

There were the raw materials—lumber, ore, and water among other things—and people of wonderful diversity and stability. Detroit had the largest percentage of people who couldn't speak English of any of America's big cities at the turn of the century but it also had more homes in proportion to its population.

And the words which a correspondent wrote in 1831 seemed equally valid in the late 1800s—and some would say even in the 1970s. Writing for an eastern newspaper, he said:

"The society of Detroit is kind, hospitable and excellent. A strong sense of equality and independence prevails in it. A citizen whose conduct is respectable and decorous is respected by all and associates with all.

"Very little etiquette is practiced here. Genuine friendliness and cordiality are agreeable substitutes . . . Recently domiciled here, we can speak feelingly upon this subject. A frank, cordial and general civility, at once peculiarly gratifying and indicative of the character of Michiganians, has been extended to us."

YOU'RE LOOKING NORTH on Woodward Avenue, from the corner of Clifford street. It's about 1875, and that cluster of trees ahead is where Grand Circus Park is located. (DHM)

DETROIT'S FIRST department store, Mabley & Co., was started in 1870 on the east side of Woodward Avenue. C. J. Mabley, the founder, later started to build a skyscraper on the corner of Michigan and Woodward, went broke in the process, and the new owners found the letter "M" (for Mabley) implanted in all sorts of corners. They solved the problem by calling it the Majestic Building. (Burton)

IT'S NOW ABOUT 1888, the horse is still king on Detroit's streets, and fashions still have a Victorian-era look. (DHM)

THEY WERE CALLED the Seventeen, and they served as young volunteers at the Children's Free Hospital on St. Antoine when this picture was taken in June, 1888. Their names? Caroline Davison, Ethel Lloyd, Alice Chaffee, Emily Meddaugh, Elizabeth Wing Noble, Mary Alice Finney, Cornelia Winder, Sarah Noble, Lulu Anita Weeks, Clara Williams, Harriette Davison, Janie Horton, Brownie Kellie, Jane Standish, Florence Annette Weeks, Nora Johnson, and Julia Mills. (UCS)

AN OUTING to Bois Blanc Island has been a thing-to-do for scores of years, as indicated by this group gathered at the river side in the 1880s. This Canadian island, on which several hundred people lived when this picture was taken, was bought by the Bob-Lo Excursion Company in the 1890s. The first excursion steamer from Detroit arrived there on Monday, June 20, 1898. It's still Bois Blanc on the map—and still Bob-Lo Island Park for thousands of Detroiters. (Burton)

ORPHANAGES WERE COMMON and this one, the Zoar Asylum of the Zion German Reformed Church, was established in 1881. It was located on Harvey Street between the River Road and Fort Street and in January, 1887, 36 orphans, 10 widows, and six men lived there. It's interesting to note that the residents were referred to as inmates. (Burton)

FIRST TOWERS ROSE TO LIGHT the streets of Detroit in the early 1880s, when it was still the custom to put out the gas and naphtha lights, then being used, whenever the moon was timed to rise, no matter what the weather. The tower in front of City Hall was 190 feet high, and others in the 100-foot range were scattered throughout the city. Some felt that the tower lamps "lighted up the heavens but not the streets" but they did give Detroit the reputation for being the best-lighted city in the country. They were in use for about 30 years. The scene is looking south on Woodward, with the Soldiers and Sailors monument on the left. The famed Russell House is on the corner now occupied by the First National Building. (Burton)

WHEN ELECTRICITY was brought to Detroiters, mutton-chopped Charles Phelps Gilbert did a lot of the work as general manager of the Edison Illuminating Company from this elaborate office of the day. He held the job from January 23, 1888 to June 26, 1896, and also had the distinction of having given Henry Ford one of his first jobs when he came to Detroit off his parents' farm. (Ford)

LATER, AS USE of electricity spread into homes, Edison came up with one of its earliest manpower-saving devices—the "Pole Raiser." (Edison)

THIS RARE VIEW OF THE CITY is a painting focusing on the Detroit Boat Club's building *(left)* in front of Parke, Davis & Co. The club moved there in 1872, later built out in the river on Belle Isle. Its oarsmen won national renown and, in 1895, competed in a regatta on the Detroit River. The painting is owned by Herbert Lott.

SCENE DURING a regatta shows 10-oared boat race just beyond Boat Club in 1895. (Burton)`

THIS NEW HOME for the Boat Club was dedicated at Belle Isle in June, 1891, with a bit of beach for youngsters nearby. It was destroyed by fire in 1893, rebuilt, destroyed by fire again in 1901, and finally replaced by the cement structure, *(opposite page, bottom)* on the river's edge in 1902. It's still home for the oldest club of its kind in the country. (Wehmeier)

WAY OUT in Highland Park, the Highland Park Railway served those who wanted to go from Detroit to the race track which was located on the spot out Woodward later filled by the Ford Motor Company. (Edison)

DETROIT'S HIGH SCHOOL, located at the site of the first State Capitol at Griswold and Gratiot, was destroyed by fire in 1893 at a time when its enrollment had passed 1,000 (above). Typical of students and faculty is this photo of the Class of 1889 (left). To be admitted, you had to be at least 12 years old and pass an examination in spelling, grammar, arithmetic, geography, reading, United States history and government. (Board of Ed.)

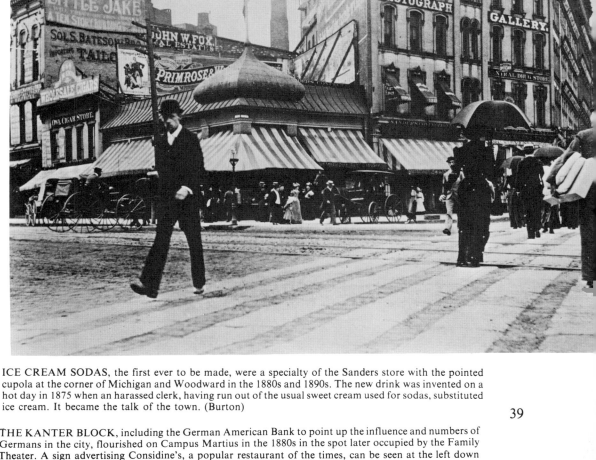

ICE CREAM SODAS, the first ever to be made, were a specialty of the Sanders store with the pointed cupola at the corner of Michigan and Woodward in the 1880s and 1890s. The new drink was invented on a hot day in 1875 when an harassed clerk, having run out of the usual sweet cream used for sodas, substituted ice cream. It became the talk of the town. (Burton)

THE KANTER BLOCK, including the German American Bank to point up the influence and numbers of Germans in the city, flourished on Campus Martius in the 1880s in the spot later occupied by the Family Theater. A sign advertising Considine's, a popular restaurant of the times, can be seen at the left down Monroe street. The Lafer Brothers store was around the corner from the bank. (Free Press)

HIGH STYLE for the 1900s was demonstrated by these women heading for the theater of an afternoon. Shoes were high-buttoned or laced, and "Merry Widow" hats with veils, bird wings and flowers were the rage. (News)

CENTRAL MARKETPLACE dominated Cadillac Square in 1890. It was built in 1880-83. The butchers had the first floor; the park, health and poor board the second; and the superior court the third. In the background is the area for the Farmer's Market. (Burton)

The Big Surge Starts
(1890-1914)

WITH ITS BUSINESS and industrial forces primed to take advantage of the still-to-be-born automotive industry, Detroit entered the 1890 decade with reform politics on its mind—and Hazen S. Pingree prepared to rout the scoundrels.

He moved from the mayor's office to the governorship of Michigan before the decade ended, and in the process achieved some changes and laid the groundwork for others. A mournful city memorialized him with a statute when he died unexpectedly in 1901. It stands in Grand Circus Park, a reminder for some at least that a liberal tradition is well rooted in Detroit's past.

By mid-1890, the first automobiles were seen on the city's streets and almost simultaneously massive new waves of immigrants began to arrive.

Racing became fashionable and there were endurance tests across the sand and mud of the countryside. Companies were formed and failed and eventually, Henry Ford, adamant in his insistence on producing cars for everyone, came up with an answer. The assembly line was born. With it in 1914 came the $5 day and the 8-hour day and the course was set. Ford built 15 million Model Ts between 1908 and 1927 and the world indeed was put on wheels by Detroiters with the ideas and skills to do it.

HAZEN S. PINGREE, who came to Detroit from Maine in 1865, helped to make it one of the largest shoe manufacturing centers in the country—and then became its reform mayor. A Republican, he was elected in 1889 by a margin of 2,300 votes in what was even then heavily-Democratic Detroit. He helped to put some officials in jail, took on the utilities, but primarily fought the streetcar franchise holders, and in 1895 inaugurated a streetcar line which introduced the three-cent fare. In 1896 he was elected governor and for a few months served as the top city and state official. The Supreme Court ruled he couldn't do that. So he chose the governorship. (DHM)

THE BIG DAY for Mayor Pingree came when he drove the first streetcar in 1895 of the new line he had pushed to compete with other franchise holders. In effect, he triggered the drive that eventually led to municipal ownership of transportation and public lighting facilities. (DHM)

THE GRAND BOULEVARD, which had been fought because it was too far out, finally was started in August, 1891, with Mayor Pingree turning the first shovel. (DHM)

PINGREE ORGANIZED his own employes to help his campaign for governor. Shown in this 1894 photo are about 100 Pingree & Smith workers, dressed in gray dusters, straw hats, and stovepipes. Pingree paid all expenses to get them to Saginaw, and employes at the factory were given $5 gold pieces for campaigning for Pingree. It wasn't until 1896 that he was nominated, however, and then he was elected. (DHM)

RUSSELL A. ALGER, a former governor of Michigan, was Secretary of War when the proclamation was signed that a state of war existed between the United States and Spain on April 21, 1898. Michigan was one of the first to respond. Its quota was four regiments of infantry, a total of 4,104 men. Some are seen here marching off to camp on Woodward Avenue. (Burton)

A MAJOR DOWNTOWN first occurred on October 7, 1897, when the Opera House on Campus Martius was destroyed. At the right can be seen smoke from one of the steam fire engines on Monroe, still pumping water to be sprayed on the ruins. (Woodard)

DETROIT WENT ALL OUT when the Grand Army of the Republic (GAR) held its national convention here in 1891. This was the climatic parade on September 6 *(left)*. In the background can be seen a great archway that was built just below Grand Circus Park as a major feature for the occasion. (Wayne)

MICHIGAN NEWSPAPER CARTOONISTS got together in 1905 to publish a 640-page collection of their drawings of leading Michigan personalities. From that book, made available by Lee Kollins, come these impressions of three of Detroit's leading businessmen of the period.

—DEXTER MASON FERRY *(left)* came to Detroit to take a job as an errand boy in 1852 and four years later, with a partner, he started a seed business which became the largest in the world. Ferry was active in many civic affairs, and other members of the family have emulated him in that regard.

—RICHARD HENRY FYFE'S *(center)* parents came to Michigan in the period of the great migrations in the late 1830s. They settled in Hillsdale and he came to Detroit in 1857 to work for a shoe merchant. By 1865, he had his own business, was manufacturing some of the finest custom shoes made in the country.

—JOSEPH LOWTHIAN HUDSON *(right)* born in England, came to Detroit from Hamilton, Ont., and worked for C. R. Mabley who established Detroit's first department store. In 1881 Hudson opened his own store in the old Detroit Opera House building, saw it develop into one of the largest retail operations in the country. (Ford)

46

BY THE TURN of the century, Detroit already had established itself as one of the more cosmopolitan cities in the country, with its variety of foreign born. Their number was to increase in the early 1900s and years later experts would be able to count as many as 85 different ethnic groups in the community. On the following pages are included pictures to point up the diversity of groups and their activities, with the realization that space is all too limited for a more comprehensive view.

WITHIN ALL GROUPS there were many efforts at mutual aid. One of the most interesting was the group of Polish farmers above. They formed a combine and bought land in the northern part of the city, which they worked together. Some of their feelings are suggested in this 1894 photo by the one sign in English and the other in Polish which, translated, says: "He who gives to others, gives to the Lord." (Wayne)

BELGIANS CLUSTERED on the East Side, and their influence is pointed up by the fact that in 1870 of 80 Catholic priests in Detroit, 53 were Belgians. In 1893, the community started the Belgian National Alliance Band and one of its sponsors was Charles Goddeeris, far left, top row, who was called the father of Belgian societies in Detroit. Goddeeris came to Detroit in 1881. (Buyse)

DRAMATIC EFFORTS were popular at the Harmonie Society, a leading German group. The scene here is of 1900 activities by actors and singers. The Harmonie Society is Detroit's second oldest club, Michigan's oldest musical group. (Keydel)

CHAPMAN ABRAHAM, Detroit's first known Jewish settler, arrived in 1762 and became a successful trader. Since that date thousands of others have followed his example—and more. Many have taken leading roles in the total community at judicial, cultural and spiritual levels, but few have had the influence exerted by Rabbi Leo M. Franklin who served Temple Beth El from 1899 to 1950. The picture shows Dr. Franklin with his first confirmation class in 1899, a class that included Retta Frank, who became Mrs. Edwin Wolf; Katherine T. Sloman, who became Mrs. Arthur Heinzelman; and Corine P. Wertheimer, who became Mrs. Herman Lewis. The boys are Sidney T. Alexander (4th from left), Jessie Grabowsky, Ira Greenbaum, Julian H. Krolik (5th from left), Herbert T. Sloman, and Joseph H. Welt (2nd from left.) (Katz)

49

GREEKTOWN HAS become one of Detroit's most popular areas, and the Hellas Cafe which was founded in 1895 by Demetrios Antonopoulos is still one of its main attractions. Antonopoulos came to the United States from Korinthos, Greece, washed dishes for a while, then opened his own place with this group of countrymen helping as waiters. The Hellas (and Greektown) is on Monroe Street on the near East side downtown.

DETROIT MEDICAL COLLEGE, from which Wayne State's medical school grew, held its first session in 1869. It was a private school and anyone was accepted "without regard to their preliminary education," and they were graduated after two sessions of five weeks each. It became city-owned in 1918. Students were hanging out of the window for a school picture *(above)* but demonstrated serious mien to watch an operation *(below)* performed at St. Mary's Hospital in 1898. Now Memorial Hospital, St. Mary's was the city's first, established in 1845 by the Sisters of Charity in the same block of buildings that were being used as a Catholic seminary. The first patient was a "poor, sick dying man, lying on a cot in an old shed." He recovered and became the hospital's first lay employe. (Wayne)

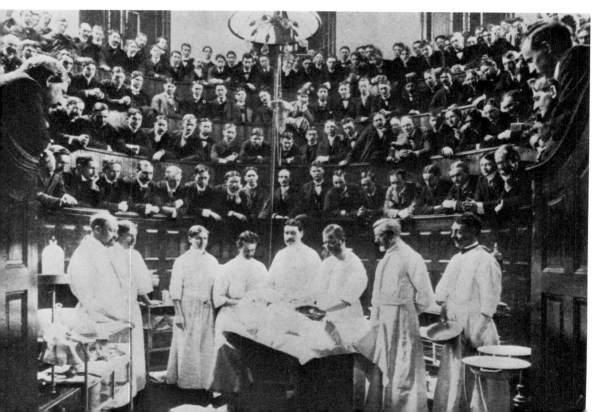

FIRST STEEL CONSTRUCTION for a building in Detroit was in the Detroit Bank & Trust's old headquarters at Gratiot and Griswold. This 1894 picture also gives some idea of construction practices of the period. Interiors were pretty stark. This one shows Sidney D. Miller, then president of the Detroit Bank, to the right of the customer's desk in 1890. Founded in 1849, the bank is the city's oldest. At the end of its first year, total deposits were $3,287. Its resources were $2,156,176,725 in 1970. (Det. Bank)

THE
Speaking Telephone!

List of Subscribers

CONNECTED WITH THE

CENTRAL OFFICE SYSTEM,

DETROIT. September 15, 1878.

CENTRAL OFFICE, No. 15 Congress St. W.

AMERICAN DISTRICT TELEGRAPH COMPANY,
OFFICE: No. 15 Congress Street West.

AMERICAN DISTRICT CARRIAGE & EXPRESS CO.,
OFFICES: No. 15 Congress Street West, and
Corner Larned and Cass Streets.

DETROIT ELECTRICAL WORKS,
OFFICE AND SALESROOM: No. 98 Griswold Street.
FACTORY: No. 207 Jefferson Avenue.

DETROIT'S FIRST "speaking telephone" was installed in 1877, but it wasn't until a year later that the first directory—4 pages with 124 names—was issued. One gets the flavor of some of the offices of the time in this view of Michigan Bell's construction center in 1913 *(facing page, below)*. By then, too, service had been enlarged with the use of giant switchboards. Detroit's first commercial installation connected the Frederick Stearns pharmacy and laboratory a half-mile away. People poured in "to throw their voices" over the device—and many remained skeptical. (Mich. Bell)

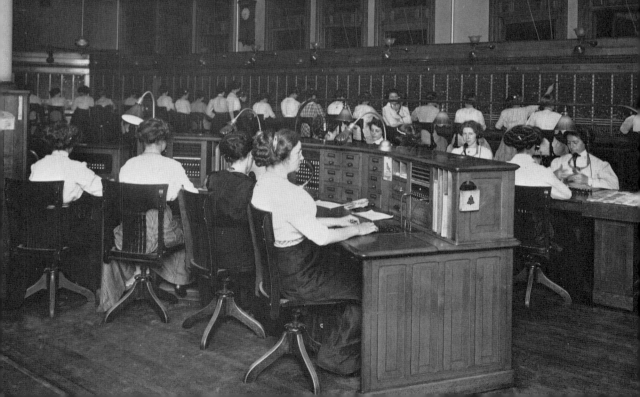

THEN CAME THE CAR, with its explosive growth and scores and scores of men with ideas and thousands and thousands of people to work in their plants. The automobile sort of evolved during the 1890s and on March 6, 1896, Charles Brady King drove the first car on the streets of Detroit. Henry Ford followed on June 6, and in 1900 Ransom E. Olds established the first production plant.

Why Detroit?

Besides being a port city, Detroit had the reputation of being the largest manufacturer of marine gas engines, and Michigan produced more carriages, buggies, and wheels than any other state. As a result, Michigan could manufacture auto bodies far below the cost in other states, and it had the metal processing plants and paint plants to provide other materials.

All this, of course, meant that a basic essential, a skilled labor force, was ready and waiting.

In 1901, a discovery in Texas and a fire in Detroit provided major impetus for development of the car and its growth in Detroit. Spindletop, a fabulous gusher, came in on January 19 near Beaumont and the price of crude petroleum dropped to less than five cents a barrel. A couple of months later the Olds plant in Detroit burned down. One model was saved, but to return to business quickly, Olds sub-contracted for parts and

HENRY FORD HELPED lead the way with this buggy chassis, mounted on four bicycle wheels, powered by an air-cooled, two-cylinder gasoline engine, and steered by a boat-like tiller. It could go forward but not backward, as Ford took this spin on a fall day in 1896 in Dearborn. (Ford)

sub-assemblies and it wasn't long before suppliers became manufacturers themselves.

There were others, too. David Buick was on his way to success enameling bathtubs when he formed the Buick Auto-Vim and Power Company which later was merged with the Flint Wagon Works and moved to Flint.

The story of how the Packard Motor Company came to Detroit, told by Robert Stoll in a Detroit Historical Society Bulletin article, points up some of the wildness of the moment. Writes Stoll:

"Henry Joy and Truman Newberry were walking along the street discussing which make of car could be cranked and started easiest. Just then, a fire engine came tearing down the street and two men ran out of a nearby building and hurriedly cranked their cars and rushed into a side street, out of the way.

'That's just the car for us,' shouted Mr. Joy, and Mr. Newberry and Mr. Joy ran after the two men to make inquiries. They liked the car so much that Mr. Joy persuaded some men to buy the Packard Company and move it from Ohio to Detroit.

Their plant on East Grand Boulevard was one of the first modern factory buildings in the world. Mr. Joy became president."

Incidentally, the Packard plant was designed by Albert Kahn, the great Detroit

54

architect, who helped revolutionize factory design and is responsible for many other outstanding Detroit buildings.

Other names began to emerge—Durant, Chapin, Dodge, Chevrolet—but basically in those early years the automobile was considered a luxury and a sporting thing. Racing became fashionable, and news of automobiles was carried on the sports pages.

It wasn't until 1904, for example, that the industry was included in U.S. census reports on manufacturing.

Ford was one of the first to visualize a world on wheels, and with his Model T of 1908 he began to move closer to the mark. In January, 1914, he started his first assembly line and a few days later, he stunned everyone with the announcement of the $5 and 8-hour day. By 1921, Ford had produced more than 5 million cars, 55.45 percent of the industry's total output at that point.

In the next few pages are some pictorial highlights to help refresh the memory of some and inform, amuse or bemuse others.

ALL CRANKED UP and ready to go are these racers of the early 1900s when automobile news was a feature of the sports pages. Included in this field are Barney Oldfield and Louis Chevrolet who later became a car builder himself. But Oldfield was the greatest of the racers. He came to Detroit as a bicycle rider and drove the Henry Ford "999" five miles in 5 minutes and 28 seconds in 1902. In 1903, he became the first human to travel a mile-a-minute in a race at the Fair Grounds in Indianapolis. "The man," said Henry Ford who is shown with him here, "did not know what fear meant." (MVMA)

FIRST BUICK MODEL was test-run from Flint to Detroit in 1904 by Chief Engineer Walter Marr, the driver, and David Buick's son, Tom. (MVMA)

FIRST DODGE was delivered to the Dodge Brothers in 1914. This picture, taken in November, shows John Dodge (bowler hat) and Horace Dodge (felt hat) in front of the John Dodge home at 75 E. Boston Boulevard. (MVMA)

CHEVROLET BUILT 2,999 cars in its first year, 1912, at its Detroit plant. Louis Chevrolet, who had won fame as a racing driver (standing left without a hat) and W. C. Durant (standing, far right, with derby) admire the first one—a six-cylinder model with folding top and adjustable windshield. The following year, Chevrolet was moved to Flint, later became part of General Motors which was organized by Durant. (GM)

PONTCHARTRAIN HOTEL was the starting point for the Glidden tour which was one of the major factors in helping to establish the industry. These long, overland competitions helped to promote interest and also served as a means of testing new equipment. The first Glidden tour of 870 miles was held in 1905. The 1909 Glidden tour from Detroit to Denver to Kansas City covered 2,636 miles (MVMA)

DIRECT DELIVERY of gasoline, from a horse-drawn tank car to a White Steamer, is handled right on the street with no problem in 1905. In 1910, the Central Oil Company built what may have been the first drive-in gasoline station with an island. The 1915 picture *(below)* at Woodward and High (now Vernor), shows what was the company's second such station. (MVMA-Burton)

57

THE LADIES seemed to enjoy this break in a cross country run. Note the limited trunk space. (MVMA)

58   AN EARLY TEST TRACK was built by Dodge in 1915 adjacent to its plant. Every car was tested before shipment for engine and brake performance on the hill, and for speed on the circular plank track. (Chrysler)

ROY CHAPIN rides an early model Hudson. He got his start with Olds, driving one of the cars to New York to prove its reliability at a time when Olds was there to arrange some financing. In 1906, Chapin joined with E. R. Thomas of Buffalo to make the Thomas-Detroit car. Later, with financial help of J. L. Hudson, he established the Hudson Motor Car Company which eventually became part of American Motors Corporation. (MVMA)

SUDDENLY—TRAFFIC. And Detroit was first with traffic lights and towers, the one shown below located at Woodward and Grand Boulevard (looking east). And, of course, there were tickets for speeders (right), the first of which, it is claimed, is being handed out in the accompanying picture. (DHM-Burton)

THIS WAS THE SPOT for the installation of the gas tank along the assembly line which was started by Henry Ford in 1914 and helped him to reach a level of 1,000 cars per day. (Ford)

60

WOMEN QUICKLY became part of the automobile industry's work force, with this group producing spark plugs at the Jeffrey-DeWitt company plant on Dubois at East Grand Boulevard. (Ford)

TRANSPORTATION was at hand when the shift broke at the Dodge Plant on Chene Street near the Boulevard. (MVMA)

HENRY AND EDSEL FORD in front of their Hendrie Street home in 1905. (Ford)

FORD FAMILY PICNIC on Belle Isle shows Edsel (third from left) sitting next to his mother, Clara Ford, with her mother, Mrs. Martha Bench Bryant, and her two sisters, Eva and Katherine, to the right. (Ford)

THEN CAME THE ROADS. This was at Grand River and West Chicago Boulevard *(above)*, and the date was April 23, 1908, when members of the Wayne County Board of Road Commissioners participated in ground-breaking ceremonies for a new pavement. First man at the plow is Edward N. Hines, who is credited with coming up with the idea of putting a white line down the center of highways. A few years later, around 1912, a County crew is seen at work *(below)* on Grand River making repairs. (Wayne)

My Farewell Car

By R. E. Olds, Designer

Reo the Fifth—the car I now bring out—is regarded by me as pretty close to finality. Embodied here are the final results of my 25 years of experience. I do not believe that a car materially better will ever be built. In any event, this car marks my limit. So I've called it My Farewell Car.

My 24th Model

This is the twenty-fourth model which I have created in the past 25 years.

They have run from one to six cylinders from 6 to 60 horsepower.

From the primitive cars of the early days to the most luxurious modern machines.

I have run the whole gamut of automobile experience. I have learned the right and the wrong from tens of thousands of users.

In this Farewell Car, I adopt the size which has come to be standard the 30 to 35 horsepower, four-cylinder car.

Where it Excels

The chiefest point where this car excels is in excess of care and caution.

The best I have learned in 25 years is the folly of taking chances.

In every steel part the alloy that I use is the best that has been discovered. And all my steel is analyzed to know that it meets my formula.

I test my gears with a crushing machine—not a hammer. I know

to exactness what each gear will stand.

I put the magneto to a radical test. The carburetor is doubly heated, for low grade gasoline.

I use nickel steel axles with Timken roller bearings.

So in every part. The best that any man knows for every part has been adopted here. The margin of safety is always extreme.

I regard it impossible, at any price, to build a car any better.

Center Control, Finish, Etc.

Reo the Fifth has a center, cane-handle control. It is our invention, our exclusive feature.

Gear shifting is done by a very slight motion, in one of four directions.

There are no levers, either side or center. Both of the brakes operate by foot pedals. So the driver climbs out on either side as easily as you climb from the tonneau.

The body finish consists of 17 coats. The upholstering is deep, and of hair-filled genuine leather.

The lamps are enameled, as per the latest vogue. Even the engine is nickel trimmed.

I have learned by experience that people like stunning appearance.

The wheel base is long the tonneau is roomy — the wheels are large—the car is over-tired. Every part of the car—of the chassis and the body—is better than you will think necessary. No price could buy anything better.

Price $1,055

This car—my finest creation has been priced for the present at $1,055.

This final and radical paring of cost is considered by most men as my greatest achievement.

It has required years of preparation. It has compelled the invention of much automatic machinery. It necessitates making every part in our factory, so no profits go to parts makers.

It requires enormous production, small overhead expense, small selling expense, small profit. It means a standardized car for years to come, with no changes in tools and machinery.

In addition to that, by making only one chassis we are cutting off nearly $200 per car.

Thus Reo the Fifth gives far more for the money than any other car in existence. It gives twice as much as some.

But this price is not fixed. We shall keep it this low just as long as we can. If materials advance even slightly the price must also advance. No price can be fixed for six months ahead without leaving big margin, and we haven't done that. The cost has been pared to the limit.

Catalog Ready

Our new catalog shows the various styles of body. It tells all the materials, gives all specifications. With these facts before you, you can easily compare any other car with this Reo the Fifth.

If you want a new car you should do that. Judge the facts for yourself. Don't pay more than our price for less value. After 25 years spent in this business, here is the best car I can build. And the price is $1,055. Don't you think you should know that car?

Write now for this catalog. When we send it we will tell you where to see the car. Address -

R. M. Owen & Co. General Sales Agents for Reo Motor Car Co., Lansing, Mich.

Canadian Factory, St. Catharines, Ontario

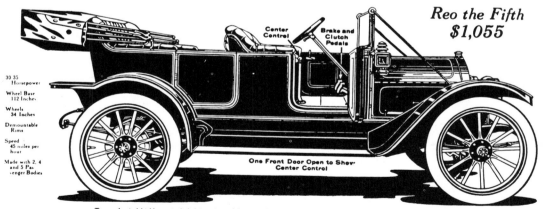

30 35 Horsepower

Wheel Base 112 Inches

Wheels 34 Inches

Demountable Rims

Speed 45 miles per hour

Made with 2, 4 and 5 Passenger Bodies

Center Control

Brake and Clutch Pedals

One Front Door Open to Show Center Control

Reo the Fifth $1,055

Top and windshield not included in price. We equip this car with mohair top, side curtains and slip-cover, windshield, gas tank and speedometer —all for $100 extra. Self-starter, if wanted, $25.00 extra.

THE ULTIMATE CAR, said Ransom E. Olds, was this Reo. In the ad, Olds says, "I do not believe that a car materially better ever will be built." Note that the extras, for $100 more than the listed price, included mohair top, side curtains and slip-cover, windshield, gas tank, and speedometer. (GM)

NOTHING OVER 10 CENTS IN THIS STORE.

189 KRESGE & WILSON, BIG 5 and 10¢ STORE 191

OUR SHEET MUSIC DEPT NOW OPEN
ALL POPULAR HITS 10 cts.
KRESGE & WILSON

OUR SHEET MUSIC DEPT NOW OPEN
ALL POPULAR HITS 10 cts.
KRESGE & WILSON

WHAT STARTED as a small 5-and-10 cent store in 1899, with merchandise hung from the ceiling, has become one of the world's largest merchandising companies. S. S. Kresge used a nestegg of $8,000 to launch the business which has now become a 4.63 billion-dollar corporation with 1,266 stores in the United States, Canada, and Australia. (Burton)

THERE WERE PLACES to go and things to do to keep one entertained in yesterday's Detroit. They ranged from strolling by the pool at Recreation Park, where the first Detroit major league baseball team played from 1881 to 1887 when it won the National League pennant, to canoeing, to skating, horseracing, and bowling.

CANOE DAY at Belle Isle attracted a large crowd on an August Sunday in 1906. (DHM)

BOWLING AND POOL was available in 1913 for those who went to Charles Lake, Mich. (DHM)

THERE WERE TROTTERS to be wagered on at the Fair Grounds in Howell in November of 1914. (Luttermoser)

BEAUTIFUL WINTER day attracted hundreds to the skating pond in Highland Park, next to the Ford plant. (Ford)

STROLLING on Central Avenue on Belle Isle was one of the more pleasant pastimes in 1902. (News)

THE DOG AND PONY show—it existed, and here's proof provided by a Wixom Bros. company.

DETROIT WAS QUICK to establish its reputation as the home-owners' capital of the country. Over the years, row on row of single homes, such as those seen here in this 1910 view of Second Avenue *(above)*, have been a trademark. Home ownership has always been at about the 70 percent level in the Detroit area. The city was not without its ghetto housing, however, as indicated by this view *(below)* of the Northwest corner of Hastings and Franklin in 1910. (Burton)

COBB AND NAVIN—two great names in Detroit baseball history—launched their careers almost simultaneously. Frank Navin joined the club as an assistant to Tom Yawkey, and wound up in 1903 owning a major interest. Ty Cobb (signing his contract here) started his first game on August 20, 1905, and wound up 20 years later having led Detroit to three pennants (1907-08-09) and having posted an incredible .369 lifetime batting average with 200 or more hits in nine seasons.

COBB WAS a great crowd pleaser on the bases, stealing as many as 96 bases in 1915, his top effort.

NAVIN, in bowler hat, even took a hand at crowd control.

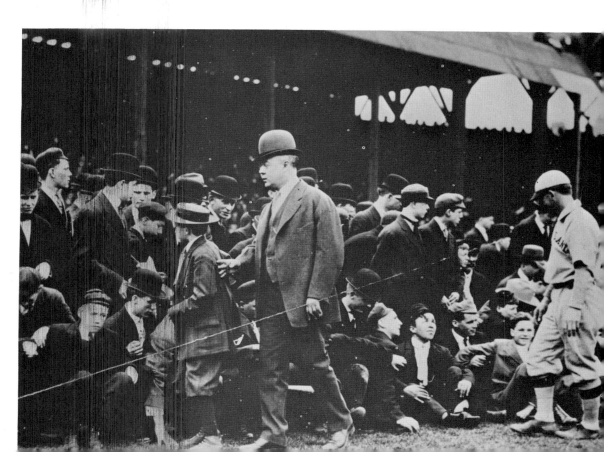

OUT AT THE FAIR there was excitement for young and old alike. This is 1894, and the Michigan State Fair which was first held in 1848, was located on grounds roughly in the area between Cass and Third from Putnam north, now occupied mostly by Wayne State University. (DHM)

DETROIT COLLEGE, from which developed the University of Detroit, included William Keane (at left) on its baseball team about 1900. Keane later was the Detroit Tigers' physician for many years. Notable, too, is the artistic effort that obviously went into posing of the team by the photographer, C.M. Mayes. (Keane)

CITY ROOM of the *Detroit Free Press* had few amenities in the early 1900s when the paper was located in a building on Lafayette near Griswold. It moved to a modern $1 million facility (now the Transportation Building) in 1913 and to its present spot in 1928. At the time of this picture which was provided by Loren Robinson, Jr., its daily circulation average for a year was 58,524, Sunday 74,408. E. D. Stair, who sold the paper to John S. Knight in 1940, was publisher. The *Detroit News,* founded in 1873, had established itself as the leading afternoon newspaper at this point and eventually became the city's only evening paper. (Free Press)

A TYPICAL DELIVERY truck of the day helped to get the *Free Press* out to street corners by morning. (MVMA)

LEADERSHIP in the movie industry has been a long-standing achievement for Detroiters. They were the first to organize movie theater owners in the country, and on this occasion in July, 1911, they gathered for a state convention in the city. Later other Detroiters organized the national exhibitors' group. (London)

DETROIT SCHOOLS were among the first to offer special education and to place emphasis on the practical. Home economics presented this somewhat primitive look of the early 1900s. Detroit's special ed department was established in 1910. Classes were provided for crippled children and for correction of speech defects. There also were open-air classes. Detroit's first kindergarten was established in 1895. (Board of Ed.)

A BRILLIANT GATHERING of Detroit artists is presented in this photo taken by Frank Scott Clark in 1912 at the famed Scarab Club. Starting from the left, seated around the first table, are: J. A. Morse, Horace Bouteil, Joseph W. Gies, Roman Kryzanowski, Louis Fett; back row, first table: another Morse, A. E. Peters, James Swain, and an unidentified man. Left to right around the second table: Roy Gamble, Clyde Burroughs, Gus Schimmel, and Charles Culver. The club, organized in 1912, has been a center of much cultural activity in Detroit. At the time of this photo, Gies who had studied in France and Germany, was considered the dean of Detroit's artists and art teachers. (Scarab)

75

THE OTTO L. LUTTERMOSER family started operating a grocery and meat market on Livernois in 1906. Going through one of the store's old ledgers, one notes such items as 3 dozen eggs for 72 cents, a loaf of bread for 7 cents, 18 pounds of sugar for $1, and 2 pounds of coffee, ground, for 40 cents. (Luttermoser)

BEFORE IT BECAME DYNAMIC, Detroit was considered the "City Beautiful" and the serenity and charm of this day in Grand Circus Park *(below)* in about 1920 was one reason. In the background is the spire of the Central Methodist Church. And for many Detroiters there were also quiet moments fishing at Conner Creek on the far East Side. The bucolic scene in 1906 *(above)* was not uncommon inside what are now Detroit's city limits. (DHM-MDCV)

From War to Depression (1914-1930)

NEWS of the $5 and 8-hour day established by Henry Ford electrified the world in 1914, and people poured into Detroit. By 1920 the population had more than doubled from 465,766 in 1910 to 993,768, and the city was the fourth largest in the country.

As dramatic as the growth in size was the change in life styles. First came the World War. The assembly lines that had been geared to provide mobility of the masses were transformed to provide the needs of the military.

Michigan adopted a prohibition law (November, 1916, to take effect May 1, 1918) and when the country caught up, it brought with it the evils of lawlessness and murder.

But the spirit of political reform triggered by Mayor Hazen S. Pingree survived. It produced a new charter in 1918 that provided for a strong mayor form of government and, in 1922, public ownership of the transit system.

Detroit would get a symphony orchestra, the beginnings of a new cultural center with the building of a library and art institute, bright new skyscrapers, among them the Fisher and Penobscot buildings, and then with the rest of the country, it would suffer the body blow of a depression.

DETROIT PARTICIPATED in three Liberty Loan drives during World War I and oversubscribed each of them by good margins. In the first year of the War, according to C. M. Burton, "Detroit sent over 43,-000 men, bought $92,242,000 in Liberty Bonds, $14,046,000 in treasury certificates, built 120 ships." Its war contracts on April 18, 1918, totaled $750,000,000. (DHM)

THE DODGE BROTHERS offered their yacht "Delphine" to the government, and this group, including Mayor Oscar B. Marx, right, was at the dock to mark the occasion. Left to right: John Dodge, Adolph Vacell, Albert A. Aldrich, unidentified Navy officer, Councilman Robert Oakman, E.T. Fitzgerald, Horace Dodge, and Marx. (Chrysler)

EVERYTHING STOPPED on November 18, 1918, when the Armistice was announced. When the boys came marching home again, crowds made it almost impossible for them to move through the downtown area.

HAMTRAMCK'S FIRST fire truck was the center of attention on this cold February day in 1915. It's parked at the southwest corner of Grayling and Joseph Campau. A few years later (1925) Joseph Campau *(below)* had taken on the appearance of neighborhood business street. (HPL)

BEFORE PROHIBITION, this Hamtramck spot was typical of the neighborhood bars in this area. (HPL)

AN UNUSUAL JEWEL for Detroit is Belle Isle which commands the juncture of Lake St. Clair and the Detroit River. The City finally purchased it in 1879 for $200,000 from Barnabas Campau in the face of strong opposition from several sources. The Island had been known as Hog Island, and with reason. A *Detroit News* writer, telling of a trip there by boat, added: "One man, armed with a big club and a rifle, had to stand constant guard over the camp to prevent depredations of the wild hogs." Frederick Law Olmstead, a distinguished designer of parks, was brought here in 1883, and from that point there began the development of the park into the major asset it is today. The first bridge, of wooden construction, shown in this superb photo by *Detroit News* photographer Bill Kuenzel, was built in 1889, destroyed by fire in 1915.

81

HOT COALS dropping from a tar wagon used during a paving job on the island fell onto creosote-soaked blocks used for the roadway on the Belle Isle bridge—and hours later on that April 27, 1915, it had been destroyed. Shown here is the fireboat Zamas Battle and other fire fighters in a futile attempt to stop the blaze. (Woodard)

THE FIRST SCARAB BALL was held in 1917 at the Addison Hotel and it became the most colorful of all social events in Detroit. Attracted, of course, was much of the city's artist colony which used to center its activity along East Jefferson Avenue. (Rypsam)

DETROIT'S charitable efforts which had depended largely on some individuals efforts in the early years, began to be organized in 1817 when "the Yankee influence" started to assert itself. A Moral and Humane Society was organized in December 1817. It lasted three years and spent $67.37 in its efforts to suppress vice and aid poor children. In February 1918, the Detroit Patriotic Fund was organized as a forerunner of the Detroit Community Fund and the United Foundation, and agencies began to be brought together for more efficient fund-raising. Among the earliest social service groups were the YWCA, the Visiting Nurses Association, and the Urban league which began to grow under the leadership of John C. Dancy. A baby clinic was among the first services provided by the League in 1919. (UCS)

PEACE AND QUIET on Washington Boulevard, *(below)* with the skeleton of the Book Building rising to the left. The "Judge William F. Connolly for Mayor" sign pinpoints the scene in 1917 when he lost to Oscar B. Marx who won his third two-year term. But then, even with a World War on, the pace of life was slow, and there was time for sitting around the fountain in the park *(above)* at Fifth and High (later Vernor Highway). (DHM)

FIRST CONVENTION BUREAU in the world was organized in Detroit in 1896 by Milton Carmichael, a reporter for the *Detroit Journal,* who found it tough convincing even the hotelmen that it was a good idea. Now practically every city has a bureau. Detroit's was given a major boost when J. Lee Barrett took over in 1914. Barrett eventually became one of the prime boosters for a Civic Center development, but in 1923 his idea was a little less dramatic. He established an information booth in Campus Martius, staffed by a score of pretty volunteers. (MDCV)

85

GROUND BREAKING for a new University of Detroit campus at the corner of Six Mile Road and Livernois took place on July 1, 1922. Six Mile Road later was renamed McNichols Road in honor of Fr. John P. McNichols, S.J., who served as U. of D.'s president from 1921 to 1932. Buildings under construction at the time of this photo were (left to right) College of Engineering, the Tower, Chemistry, Commerce and Finance, now home of the College of Business and Administration. U. of D. was founded in 1877, started in a house on East Jefferson by Jesuits, and was called Detroit College. (U. of D.)

A NEW CENTER for Detroit was started with the construction of the 15-story General Motors Building in 1920. It's the company's world headquarters and contains 20 million cubic feet of office space. With the Fisher Building including a theater, across the street, and the Burroughs company headquarters nearby, the GM building helps form one of the city's major business and entertainment sections, just four miles north of Downtown. (GM)

UNUSUAL NUMBER of General Motors leaders is brought together in this photograph taken at Anderson, Indiana, May 15, 1928. They had gone there to meet with C.E. Wilson (center, first row) who was general manager of Delco-Remy Division at the time. He became GM president in 1941. Left to right (front row) George Whitney, Junius S. Morgan, Jr., Alfred P. Sloan, Jr. (then president of GM), Wilson, William S. Knudsen (later also president), Walter S. Carpenter, Jr., and Samuel McLaughlin. Second row (left to right): Charles Kettering, Donaldson Brown, Henry M. Crane, Charles S. Mott, and Earle P. Johnson. (GM)

THE LAST OF THE BIG 3 automobile companies was formally organized in 1925, but Walter P. Chrysler, the man who put it all together, had been a major figure in the industry for some time. He started as a railroad man in Kansas, wound up as works manager for Buick Motor in Flint in 1912, and later became president of that company and a General Motors vice president. He retired at 45 but soon was back in the business, and eventually introduced his first Chrysler with a revolutionary, six-cylinder, high-compression engine in January 1924. Chrysler launched the Plymouth and bought Dodge Brothers Inc. in 1928. (Chrysler)

THE HAPPY WARRIOR, Alfred E. Smith, who would be the Democratic candidate for President in 1928, visited Walter P. Chrysler at his Jefferson avenue plant in 1925. (Chrysler)

87

RECRUITING DEALERS was a basic concern for all automobile companies, and Chrysler did its bit with this major meeting in Chicago in 1929. (Chrysler)

RED CROSS LADIES provided a colorful touch with their formation in a great Liberty Bond Parade in September, 1918, as the climax of World War I approached. Huge crowds lined the curb for blocks in this effort to stimulate interest in bond-buying. Detroit always surpassed its quota. (Red Cross)

OSSIP GABRILOWITSCH, right, listens while Walter Chrysler, next to him, discusses something with Albert Kahn, Detroit's distinquished architect, and an unidentified man at a mid-1920s gathering. (Chrysler)

IT WAS NOT UNTIL 1914 that Detroit had its first Symphony Orchestra, shown above with Weston Gales as its conductor. It played its first concert on February 26 in the Grand Opera House on Campus Martius. In 1918, when the directors decided to make a permanent appointment and picked Ossip Gabrilowitsch, he insisted on one thing: that they provide a new hall. They did at Woodward and Parsons, but in the depression years, support for the Orchestra faded and Orchestra Hall became a movie house. It was later abandoned and still later made the object of a drive to save it. Its acoustics are considered unparalleled. (Musicians Union)

89

AT THE START, Detroiters played important roles in the development of the airplane industry. William
B. Stout designed the first all-metal plane which Henry Ford put into production in 1925, and Charles E.
Lindbergh, whose feat of crossing the Atlantic was critical to ending a lot of peoples' fears and giving a
boost to commercial aviation, was born here. He stopped at the Ford Airport with his Spirit of St. Louis
(above) before flying East for his memorable solo flight to Paris that ended on May 20, 1927. With him
(below) was his mother, Mrs. Evangeline Land Lindbergh who taught at Cass Tech at the time. (Ford)

BIG BOOST FOR AIR TRAVEL came with the start of the Airplane Reliability Tours in 1925. Sparked by the Detroit Chamber of Commerce, the tour idea was designed to emphasize that air travel could be safe. Up to that time the spotlight had been on the military and the thrill and stunt flyers. The first tour, including 16 planes, was a 1,775-mile test, starting from the Ford Airport on September 28, 1925. Shown in the picture is part of the crowd that was on hand on a gloomy, rainy day when the planes completed their tour. Eleven of them made it. Ford also became involved in the building of planes with William B. Stout, who started one of the first regularly scheduled airlines. By 1931, Ford lost interest, and what might have been a major industry in Detroit faded. At right is the Ford Reliability Trophy.

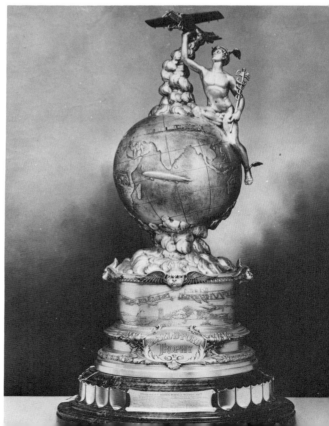

AIR-MINDED DETROITERS scored another coup when they brought the 16th Gordon Bennett trophy race to Detroit in 1927. Fifteen balloons representing 8 nations were here for the event, which was won by the Detroit entry. Shown here is the start of the race on September 10, 1927, and among the spectators was a chubby Henry Ford II *(below)* who is shielding his eyes from the sun as the balloons begin to soar. (Ford)

THE *Detroit News,* interestingly enough, helped to make aviation history in Detroit when famed photographer Bill Kuenzel provided its readers with the first aerial pictures of Detroit in 1912. Years later, on a bright February Sunday in 1931, more than 100,000 people surrounded the Detroit City Airport (which had been opened on October 24, 1927) to see the *Detroit News* Autogiro perform. The paper used that equipment for about 2½ years to transport reporters and photographers to stories. It later also used a company plane for the same purpose. (News)

93

HISTORIC AIRPLANE is viewed by Detroiters at the Michigan State Fair in 1925. The first plane of the
Ford Air Transportation Service flew from Detroit to Chicago on April 13, 1925, carrying 1,000 pounds
of mail and small parts for the Ford Chicago plant. It took this "Tin Goose" two hours and 52 minutes
for the flight, which was another among those that helped to give Detroit an historic role in aviation.

ONE FORD PLANE caught another in this aerial picture of Detroit taken on September 15, 1927. This
was one of about 100 tri-motors built here before the company decided to drop out of the airplane
business in the early 1930s. (Ford)

HARVEY CAMPBELL, who for years was the city's "Mr. Detroit" as president of the Board of Commerce, wound up in jail in 1928—and was "damned proud" of it. The city was involved in a condemnation suit for a strip of property between Memorial and Owen parks. When Judge Edward Jeffries came down with an award, Campbell blasted Jeffries, contending it was too high. He wound up with a 15-day sentence for contempt. Later the award was cut down by $1.5 million and Campbell figured that his prison term was worth $100,000 a day to the city. He ran the Board of Commerce from 1919 until he retired in 1962, was fond of saying: "Anybody can make anything but everybody can't sell." (Free Press)

CLARENCE DARROW (right) provided one of the first dramatic moments for Detroit civil rights supporters when he came to defend Henry Sweet (left) who had been charged with murder. Sweet's brother, Dr. Ossian Sweet, had moved into a home in the solidly-white East Side in September 1925, and Henry was with Ossian and his family when a crowd gathered and started throwing rocks. Shots were fired from within the house, killing one person. Ossian Sweet and 10 others, including Henry, were charged with murder. In the first trial of 11 persons, with Darrow also leading the defense, the jury deadlocked. In April 1926, Henry Sweet stood trial alone. Darrow came back and won his acquittal. Each time Darrow made much in his charge to the juries of the racism that pervaded the community. Attorneys Julian Perry and Tom Chawkes are between Sweet and Darrow. (Wayne)

95

FROM THE DAC (Detroit Athletic Club) located on Madison at the left of the Hotel Tuller bounded by Adams on the right, one can see the heart of Detroit in the mid-1920s *(above)*. Dramatically pointed up is the spoke-like effect of the streets coming off the Grand Circus Park semicircle, at the bottom of the picture. (MDCV)

FURTHER NORTH, the Main Library on the left and the Detroit Institute of Arts were bright, new additions to the city, and the start of what would become the Cultural Center. (MDCV)

FIRES HAVE RAVAGED the city from time to time, starting with the big one in 1805. Whole blocks were burned thereafter as the city moved from bucket-brigade type fire fighting (the last time in 1837) to more modern equipment. In 1848, a quarter of the city and most of the business district went up in flames on May 9. However, few lives ever were lost until an explosion in the *Detroit Journal* building on November 6, 1895, killed 37, the largest loss in a single fire in the city's history. On April 23, 1927, the Briggs Manufacturing plant burned down, with the loss of 21 lives *(above)*. It was the city's first $2 million fire. The Study Club fire in 1929 when 22 died and the Export Box fire in 1945, killing 21, were other major catastrophes. (Free Press)

WITH PROHIBITION came the gangs, and one of the most notorious of them was the Purple Gang which flourished in the late 1920s and early 1930s. This police photo, introduced in evidence in a Detroit trial, is one of the rare times when most of the group was brought together. Rum-running, blind pigs, and murder were the order of the day while Detroiters were able to get cheap and imported beer and whiskey with little real problem. Many places simply pulled down the shades and went on operating when prohibition came, pulled them back up when it was ended in 1933. Michigan was the first state to pass a prohibition law and the first one to ratify the act that finally ended it.

"THE BROWN DERBY CLUB . . . had nothing to do with Al Smith's . . . headgear," wrote Malcolm Bingay, editor of the *Free Press* in the 1930s, in his biography. The actual club consisted of nine members: Peter J. Monaghan, Edwin Kerwin, Robert Rahaley, Emmett Sheahan, William M. Dillion, Dr. William E. Keane, David H. Crowley, Havelock, Northmore and Bingay. They were former Corktowners—eight fourth-degree Knights of Columbus and one 33rd-degree Mason (Bingay). They used to fish and generally enjoy themselves as suggested in this picture provided by Leontine Keane, daughter of Dr. Keane who for many years was the Detroit Tigers' trainer.

DETROIT HAD FEW sports heroes in the 1920s but one of them, Walter Hagen, made up for it with his colorful personality and outstanding golfing ability. Hagen dominated the pros from 1914 to 1933. He won his third British Open in 1928, then headed for Hollywood to make a picture, "Green Grass Widows" with Hedda Hopper (below, at left) and Gertrude Olmstead. He also made headlines when divorcing his wife, the former Edna Strauss (left), whom he had married in 1923. (Free Press)

THE DUCHARME MANSION which was at the corner of Chene and East Jefferson was the site of this costume affair in 1927. Artist Art Jaegger who had his studio there, played host. The Raggedy-Ann couple at the left are Mr. and Mrs. Fred Rypsam and the Russ Legges are the couple next to the gent in the Indian mask in the lower left hand corner. Others in the picture include Ralph Holmes, critic for the *Detroit Times;* Art Marschner, a *Detroit News* artist, and Oscar Klausner, who won fame as a skater. (Rypsam)

FEW REALIZE that over the years Detroit has been one of America's leading popular music centers. Jerome H. Remick's company was number one in producing sheet music in the early 1900s, being responsible for such songs as "Shine on Harvest Moon," "When You Wore a Tulip," "Till We Meet Again," and "Japanese Sandman" among others. There have been many great musical names from Detroit but one of the best remembered is Jean Goldkette whose orchestra helped to enliven the Arcadia and Graystone Ballrooms in Detroit and other dance halls around the country. Among the famous musicians who played in his bands were Bix Beiderbecke, Frankie Trumbauer, Tommy and Jimmy Dorsey, Russ Morgan, Joe Venuti, Eddie Lang, Doc Ryker, Fuzzy Ferrar, Charles Margolis, and on and on. (Musicians Union)

AN ERA WAS ENDING. This pleasant picture of a string quartet posed amidst ferns in the hall of the Dickinson School in Hamtramck in 1928 serves as a reminder. Cecelia Czernecki was the violist, Mary Sokoluk, first violin; Mitchell Osadczuk, second violin, and Joe Kazakvich, cello. (HPL)

JOE CLARK caught something of the spirit of industrial Detroit and its river when he captured this moment with sea gulls in flight. (HPL).

102

The Incredible 1930s

IT MIGHT WELL be dubbed the "Incredible Thirties"—a decade that started in despair and ended with a challenge to Detroit to provide once again the arms America needed for a World War.

There were some incongruities in the city's role as it swung from the poignancy of economic defeat to the ecstasy of athletic—and some would add social—triumphs.

For the 1930s was a time when at one moment there was news of the recall of a mayor, a major murder, or the shocking word that Detroit's banks were the first in the country to close, and the next news of a new title being won to make it the City of Champions. One moment there was the bitterness of a strike, the next settlements that helped to set the pattern for more than a few advances in labor management relationships around the world.

Prohibition ended with Michigan the first to ratify repeal on April 3, 1933, and new political forces began to move to the center of the stage as Democrats began an era of domination.

WITH THE START of the decade and the inauguration of Mayor Charles Bowles *(above)*, Detroit was hit with a rash of gangland murders, Jerry Buckley, the radio commentator of the day, charged corruption in the administration and helped to bring about a recall election in which citizens voted out Bowles on July 22. At 1 a.m. on July 23, hours after the result was known, Buckley was shot to death as he sat in the lobby of the LaSalle Hotel (now Carmel Hall). Thousands went to his funeral, and even a year later additional thousands were on hand for a memorial service at the Belle Isle Shell. Mayor Frank Murphy spoke. Added excitement surrounded the trial of Ted Pizzino, Angelo Livecchi and Joe Bommarito who were charged with the murder. Famed Attorney Anthony Maiullo defended the trio, saw them acquitted after a brilliant 7-hour summation in the trial before Judge Edward Jeffries *(left)*. Maiullo *(below)* is shown perusing a brief at the far right.

OVER AND UNDER THE RIVER, there was great excitement in the late 1920s when work began on the Windsor Tunnel and the mile-long Ambassador Bridge, one of the longest suspension bridges in the world. It opened for traffic on November 15, 1929, and the tunnel was operative on November 3, 1930. (MDCV)

TREES HANGING from the roof were part of this unusual exhibit featuring 1930 General Motors models. This show at the Astor Hotel in New York was a predecessor of GM's Motoramas of the 1950s, and dramatizes the lengths to which manufacturers have gone to promote their products. (GM)

BITTER CONTROVERSY developed in the early 1930s when the Detroit Art Institute, with the help of a contribution by Edsel Ford, brought in Diego Riviera, the noted Mexican artist, to create four murals in what was a garden court. They were powerful in their depiction of Detroit's industrial life, and some accused Riviera of injecting Communist ideology into his portrayal. There was talk of whitewashing them—which fortunately never happened. (DIA)

THE FIRST ART show held in Detroit in 1883 attracted 176,456 in 20 days—and convinced a lot of people that the city was ready for a museum. James Scripps, who had founded the *Detroit News* just a few years earlier, led in fund-raising and later was generous with his gifts, as evidenced by this Scripps collection displayed in 1904 which includes Murillo's "Immaculate Conception." (DIA)

FEW PEOPLE have proved to be more generous patrons of Detroit's art museum than Mr. and Mrs. Edsel Ford, shown here at a 1935 reception with Dr. William R. Valentiner, the museum's director from 1922 to 1945. It was Valentiner who met Diego Riviera on the West Coast and convinced him to come to Detroit to produce the unusual murals, and Edsel Ford provided the financial support. (Free Press)

ONE EXPLOSION in the 1930s that was fun was provided by the American Legion convention which brought thousands of veterans to Detroit in 1931. There were plenty of hijinks but on this occasion the fellows were taking time out at Olympia to hear a speech by President Herbert Hoover. (News)

TESTIMONIAL DINNER IN HONOR OF
MAYOR DR. R. G. TENEROWICZ
SPONSORED BY
LADIES CIVIC LEAGUE HAMTRAMCK MICH.
APRIL 26-1930
HOFFMAN STUDIOS
5456 CHENE ST.

HAMTRAMCK TURNED out in force for this dinner honoring Dr. Rudolph G. Tenerowicz who was one of the city's most colorful political figures for years. He served four terms as mayor, was convicted on

110

a vice-ring conspiracy charge in 1934, was pardoned by Gov. William Comstock, then ran and was elected to Congress for two terms. He actively practiced medicine throughout his life. (HPL)

ADULT EDUCATION has always been a factor in the plans of the Detroit school system. Special classes have been made available to newcomers, whether from the South or from foreign lands. Courses have been in the English language and other skills needed for them to adjust to their new surroundings. These 1931 pictures show a summer evening class meeting in the library of the Delray Presbyterian Church *(above)* and an afternoon session at the Maybee Elementary school. (Board of Ed.)

WHEN THE DEPRESSION began to be deeply felt, Detroiters reacted, and the result was protest meetings and tragedy. Four men were killed at the climax of a hunger march at the Rouge plant on March 7, 1932, and thousands turned out to walk in the funeral procession a few days later. And while George White's Scandals were being presented in the Opera House *(below)*, a Communist demonstration tied up traffic on the Campus Martius a few weeks later. (Wayne)

113

EIGHT-DAY HOLIDAY FOR ALL BANKS IN MICHIGAN

DETROIT TIMES

CITY EDITION | **EXTRA**

33D YEAR, NO. 137   DETROIT, MICHIGAN, TUESDAY, FEBRUARY 14, 1933   24 PAGES   THREE CENTS

Proclamation Closing Banks to Protect State

Whereas, in view of the acute financial emergency now existing in the city of Detroit and throughout the state of Michigan, I deem it necessary in the public interest and for the preservation of the public peace, health and safety, and for the equal safeguarding without preference of the rights of all depositors in the banks and trust companies of this state and at the request of the Michigan Bankers' Association and the Detroit Clearing House and after consultation with the banking authorities, both national and state, with representatives of the United States Treasury Department, the Banking Department of the State of Michigan, the Federal Reserve Bank, the Reconstruction Finance Corporation, and with the United States Secretary of Commerce, I hereby proclaim the days from Tuesday, February 14th, 1933, to Tuesday, February 21st, 1933, both dates inclusive, to be public holidays during which time all banks, trust companies and other financial institutions conducting a banking or trust business within the state of Michigan shall not be opened for the transaction of banking or trust business, the same to be recognized, classed and treated and have the same effect in respect to such banks, trust companies and other financial institutions as other legal holidays under the laws of this state, provided that it shall not affect the making or execution of agreements or instruments in writing or interfere with judicial proceedings. Dated this 14th day of February, 1933, 1:32 a.m.

WILLIAM A. COMSTOCK, Governor of the State of Michigan.

ERNIE SCHAAF SUCCUMBS TO BRAIN OPERATION AFTER KNOCKOUT

NEW YORK, Feb. 14.—Ernie Schaaf, Boston boxer knocked unconscious in his bout with Primo Carnera Friday night, died at Polyclinic Hospital at 4:20 o'clock this morning.

Mortgage Holiday Asked in Nebraska

LINCOLN, Neb. Feb. 14.—Gov. Charles W. Bryan today issued an "emergency" proclamation, in which he asked farm and home mortgage holders to suspend all foreclosures until Congress and the state Legislature and a board of conciliation can act.

Banking Holiday Here Ties Up 720 Million

Pupils on deposit in Detroit banks, according to statements of December 31, 1932, were:

First National Bank, Detroit	$415,587,907
Guardian National Bank of Commerce	101,972,954
Detroit Savings Bank	54,911,800
Commonwealth Commercial State Bank	13,000,822
Peoples Wayne County Bank	11,833,904
Industrial Morris Plan Bank	1,600,617
Dime Bank	19,130,983
Union Guardian Trust Company	15,159,185
Equitable Trust Company	1,519,665
	$715,891,202

War Supply Bill Hiked $24,000,000

WASHINGTON, Feb. 14.—The War Department supply bill, carrying a total of $373,000,000 in appropriations for the next fiscal year, $24,000,000 more than the House bill, was approved by the Senate. An amendment by Senator Couzens, appropriating $22,000,000 for the care of homeless youths was included.

Prisoner Is Slain By Fellow Convict

HUNTSVILLE, Tex. Feb. 14.—Clyde Thompson, who admittedly killed two boys in Eastland County in 1928 just to see them kick," and whose death sentence was commuted to life imprisonment, today was listed by state prison officials as the slayer of a third man, this time a fellow convict.

Utility Chief Took Life, Coroner Says

CHARLOTTE, N. C., Feb. 14.—Death of Roy L. Peterman, vice-president of the Southern Public Utilities Co., was pronounced a suicide by a coroner's jury. Peterman was found shot to death in his home Saturday night.

Lay $230,000 Theft To High School Boy

OMAHA, Neb. Feb. 14.—Ray Winger 18-year-old high school student was to be returned to Idaho today to answer charges of stealing $230,000 of state bonds.

STATEMENTS BY OFFICIALS

GOVERNOR COMSTOCK

"At 3 p.m. Monday, February 13, I was requested by telephone to reach Detroit from Lansing at the earliest possible moment to take part in an important conference relative to the general banking situation. This conference was precipitated by an unforeseen and acute situation which had suddenly arisen in the affairs of one of our leading financial institutions, the Union Guardian Trust Company.

"It was the consensus of opinion after long conference by those present that the difficulties might be ironed out provided time could be had for negotiations. As matters stood it would have been necessary to close the doors of the institution involved on the morning of February 14th, which would likely bring in its train disaster to many others of our banking institutions in Michigan.

Crisis Caused by Threatened Withdrawals and Frozen Assets

"The crisis was caused by the inability to realize immediately upon the assets of the institution to meet threatened withdrawals. For the protection of smaller depositors in our institutions and to prevent the withdrawal of large sums from the state of Michigan it was deemed wise to declare a banking holiday for a period sufficiently long to allow the situation to be cleared up.

"The conference was participated in by representatives of all clearing house banks of Detroit, representatives of the Michigan Bankers Association, Secretary of Commerce of the United States Roy D. Chapin, Undersecretary of the United States Treasury Arthur A. Ballantine, the deputy governor of the Federal Reserve Bank for the seventh district, the chief national bank examiner for the seventh district, representatives of the Reconstruction Finance Corporation and the Michigan Banking Commission.

"I am convinced that the action taken is in the best interest of the people of this state and especially the smaller depositors in our banking institutions.

Gives Federal Agencies Time To Work Out Stabilizing Plans

ROY D. CHAPIN
Secretary of Commerce

"After discussion of the Detroit banking situation with the various authorities in Washington, the undersecretary of the Treasury, Arthur A. Ballantine, and I came to Detroit Saturday to co-operate with the Detroit bankers here. Certain conditions had developed in which Detroit bankers deemed assistance of federal agencies necessary. The requirements as well as the time involved to arrange all the details, whom were changing rapidly, made it seem wise to the bankers and to us that a public holiday be requested of Governor Comstock. He has seen fit to declare this and during its period an opportunity is provided to work out plans which we hope will stabilize the entire Michigan situation."

Under Secretary of Treasury Pledges Fullest Aid of U. S.

ARTHUR A. BALLANTINE
Undersecretary of the Treasury

"From close contact during some days with phases of the banking situation existing in this state I believe that Governor Comstock acted very wisely in making his declaration of public holidays. All agencies of the federal government touching the banking field have been giving closest attention and fullest support to these state problems. The time available proved to be too short for final solutions, but further time and effort should be productive of constructive results. The governor's action gives opportunity for this."

All Detroit Banks and Trust Companies to Close for Holiday

"In accordance with the proclamation of Governor Comstock, declaring a bank holiday during the period from Feb. 14, 1933, to Feb. 21, 1933, and believing it to be in the best interests of the financial and business institutions of the state of Michigan, all Detroit banks and trust companies will not be open for business until termination of the holiday proclaimed by the governor."

This statement was made by Detroit banks and trust companies and also by the Michigan Bankers Association for banks and trust companies throughout the state.

Appeal From Detroit Bankers For Eight-Day Breathing Spell

"In this excellency, the governor of the state of Michigan:

"In view of the acute financial emergency now existing in the city of Detroit and throughout the state of Michigan, we

(Continued on Next Page, Col. 5)

UNION GUARDIAN TRUST CO. DIFFICULTY CAUSES ORDER; BRINGING U. S. AID

Governor William A. Comstock at 3 o'clock this morning issued a proclamation closing all banks, trust companies and all other financial institutions in Michigan for an eight-day period from February 14 to February 21 inclusive.

This action, ties up for at least a week, $650,523,979 in deposits in Detroit banks alone. In addition, $71,567,808 of trust deposits are impounded.

About 500 banks and trust companies are affected by the bank holiday.

Governor Comstock, in a signed statement, announced the bank holiday in Michigan was due to difficulties in which the Union Guardian Trust Company found itself.

"It was the consensus of opinion," the governor asserted, "that the difficulties might be ironed out, provided time could be had for negotiations.

The governor's statement said the Union Guardian Trust Company would have had to close its doors today, and it was in fear this step would cause disaster to other banking

(Continued on Next Page, Col. 1)

114

ON SAINT VALENTINE'S DAY in 1933, Detroit suffered its bitterest blow when Governor Comstock issued a proclamation *(opposite page)* closing all banks. He signed it at 1:32 A.M. that day, and the next morning people gathered at their banks, stunned by the news. Business was paralyzed, and the crisis hit bottom when President Roosevelt closed all banks in the country on March 6. By March 21, Michigan banks began to open again, but city government was so hard hit that it began to issue scrip *(above)* to meet its payrolls. Out of it, of course, came the Federal Deposit Insurance laws. (Wayne-Det. Bank)

RARE IS THE WORD for this photograph which shows two of Detroit's distinguished father-and-son teams—James Couzens and Frank and Henry Ford and Edsel. Couzens bought into the original Ford company for $2,000 in 1903, and Ford bought him out in 1919 for $29,308,857, and their relations were not very amicable thereafter. James Couzens became Detroit's leading philanthropist. He served as Mayor from 1919 to 1922 when he was appointed United States Senator, and his son Frank served as Mayor between 1933 and 1937. This picture was taken in March, 1933, at a time when Henry Ford and Senator Couzens differed profoundly on the handling of the bank closure. Frank Couzens was Mayor at the time. (Ford)

116

FEW INDIVIDUALS were to make a greater impact on the city in the 1930s than the Rev. Charles E. Coughlin. He started broadcasting from his Shrine of the Little Flower in the 1920s, built up a reputation for being for the little guy, then began to lose his hold on what at one time was supposed to be 5 million followers when he began to attack President Roosevelt, calling him a "liar." He was forced off the air in the early 1940s by Bishop Mooney. (Free Press)

SOME IDEA OF HOW political power was concentrated in Detroit in November, 1933, is demonstrated in this gathering which includes Acting Mayor John W. Smith, and (from left to right), Congressman Carl M. Weideman, Corporation Counsel Raymond J. Kelly, Joseph Koski, secretary to Congressman George G. Sadowski, Sadowski, Public Works Commissioner Laurence G. Lenhardt, and Congressman John Lesinski. They were discussing plans prior to heading for Washington to seek aid for the unemployment crisis of that day. (Free Press)

WHEN GARFIELD ARTHUR (GAR) WOOD defended the Harmsworth Trophy in a race on the Detroit River in 1931, he started a series of sports victories involving Detroiters that soon had people talking of "The City of Champions." Wood won the trophy in 1920 with his first Miss America. He defended in a disputed race with Kaye Don in 1931, then defeated Don and his Miss England III in 1932, and Hubert Scott-Paine in 1933. Wood moved to Detroit in 1914, after inventing the hydraulic lift which made him a millionaire. But he usually had time for one of Detroit's oldest charities—the Old Newsboys Goodfellow newspaper sale. He's shown participating in 1936.

EDDIE TOLAN added a double-victory in the 1932 Olympics to the list of great Detroit performances. A graduate of Cass Tech and the University of Michigan, Tolan (center) defeated Ralph Metcalfe (left) in the 100 and 200-meter races and became the second Detroiter and third University of Michigan grad to score an Olympic double. Archie Hahn, another Detroiter, did it in 1904 and Ralph Craig in 1912. (Free Press)

DETROIT'S DRIVE to the pennant in 1934 had everything, including a love story. Pitcher Lynwood (Schoolboy) Rowe played the leading role in both respects. He won 16 straight games and a wife, Edna, in the process. One day while being interviewed on radio, Schoolboy quite offhandedly remarked "How'm ah doing, Edna." Edna? Who's Edna? Well, Detroit's press made sure that everyone knew about Edna Mary Skinner and soon reporters, photographers, and editors were trying to outdo each other with this romance of the century. Poor Edna found herself suddenly dragged out of the relative calm of El Dorado, Arkansas, into the maelstrom of a wild Detroit pennant drive. After the 1934 World Series—which the Tigers lost to St. Louis—Edna and Lyn were married with Teammate Peter Fox and his wife as attendants at a quiet ceremony.

MICKEY COCHRANE was the sparkplug who ignited the Tigers and the town in 1934. Typical of his play is this shot *(above)* of him tagging out Wally Moses in a game against the Philadelphia Athletics on June 15, 1935. Cochrane was a fiery type fellow whose career was ended after he was hit on the head by a pitched ball in 1937, but not before he had led Detroit to two successive pennants and its first World Series victory in 1935. Goose Goslin got the hit, Pitcher Tommy Bridges the victory, and both got a hug from Frank Navin *(left)* after the 7th game victory over the Chicago Cubs that triggered a wild ticker-tape response in the downtown area. (Free Press)

119

JUST A FEW WEEKS after the Detroit Tigers had won the World Series in 1935, the city went wild again when the Detroit Lions beat the New York Giants, 26 to 7, for the National Football League championship. The Lions came to Detroit in 1934, led by a couple of Clarks—Potsy the coach and Dutch the great all-around back. It didn't take them long to win popularity. On Thanksgiving Day 1934, 26,000

DUTCH CLARK glides past Chicago Bears tackler George Wilson during their 1934 game. Both Clark and Wilson, later, were to coach the Lions. (Lions)

ETROIT LIONS vs. CHICAGO BEARS
THANKSGIVING DAY 1934
ATTENDANCE 26,000
APPROX. 20,000 TURNED AWAY

turned out to see them play the Chicago Bears at University of Detroit stadium, and thousands more were turned away. With Dutch Clark in that backfield were Ernie Caddel, Ace Gutowsky, and Frank Christiansen. The players' payoff for winning the title game that year was $288. (Lions)

"ON THE ROAD, we used to stop the team bus and practice in any convenient vacant field," Aid Kushner, the former Lions' trainer, told the author one day. In this picture of his, Dutch Clark is handling the ball during a practice session at Chandler Park, their home base in 1934.

Practice at Chandler Park 1934

LITTLE DID THEY KNOW that a few months after this picture was taken in November, 1935, Manager Jack Adams *(left)* and Detroit Red Wings Captain Herbie Lewis would be savoring a Stanley Cup victory. The Wings also won ice hockey's most-prized trophy in 1936-37 to keep alive the "City-of-Champions" mystique.

122

JOE LOUIS *(right)* completed the Detroit sports story when he finally won the world heavyweight championship by beating Jim Braddock in June 1937, after having dominated the ring for a couple of years, Julian Black and John Roxborough *(below,* at left) were hailed for their part in bringing Joe along to the top. (Free Press)

JOE LOUIS' mother, Mrs. Lilly Reese Brooks (Joe's father, Munn Barrow, died when Joe was four) became a neighborhood heroine in the East side area where Joe grew up. (Free Press)

TWO MOMENTS are particularly memorable in the Louis saga—the knockout suffered by Joe Louis at the hands of Max Schmeling of Germany in 1936 and his revenge kayo on June 22, 1938 *(below)*. Ringsiders said Joe threw 41 punches in that one and had Schmeling screaming in pain. (Free Press)

THE YEAR 1937 WAS HISTORIC in the drive for industrial unionization. First there was the settlement of the sit-down strike at General Motors in Flint which was followed by a walkout at Cadillac *(above)*, led by Walter Reuther and other United Auto Workers officials of that time. And there was a sit-in at Chrysler that produced a "ticker tape" shower at one point. (Wayne)

HOMER MARTIN *(left),* first president of the UAW, addressed one of the largest crowds ever massed in Cadillac Square *(below)* for a rally in March, 1937. Wyndham Mortimer (to his left) and Ed Hall, UAW vice presidents, listened with grim attention. (Wayne)

125

STRIKE VOTE!!

By order of the vote of the Union last Sunday, a STRIKE VOTE will be taken at our regular meeting, called for

SUNDAY, MAY 5, 1935
1:00 P. M.

at POLISH FALCON HALL, 4130 Junction Avenue

It is the DUTY and PRIVILEGE of all employees to attend this meeting, inasmuch as the results of the vote will affect ALL OF YOU. Every employee of the Kelsey-Hayes Wheel Company will have an opportunity to be heard. Many of you have had plenty to say in the past. Come and say it now, where it will mean something.

The vote taken at this meeting will be governed by the the old AMERICAN principle of MAJORITY RULE.

Come and say what you have to say NOW!
LATER WILL BE TOO LATE!!

Sponsored by Educational Committee of Federal Labor Union No. 18677, A. F. of L.

GŁOSOWANIE W SPRAWIE STRAJKU!

Decyzja zapadła na zebraniu unji, jakie odbyło się ubiegłej niedzieli, aby głosowanie w sprawie strajku odbyło się na naszem regularnem zebraniu. Zebranie, na którem odbędzie się głosowanie nad strajkiem, odbędzie się w NIEDZIELĘ, 5-go MAJA o godzinie 1-ej po południu w Sokolni, 4130 Junction Avenue.

Jest obowiązkiem i przywilejem każdego z robotników być na tem zebraniu, gdyż głosowanie, jakie się tam odbędzie, będzie dotyczyć WAS WSZYSTKICH. Każdy robotnik z Kelsey-Hayes Wheel Co. będzie miał sposobność, na tem zebraniu, wypowiedzieć swoje zdanie. Wielu z was miało wiele do powiedzenia w przeszłości. Przyjdźcie na to zebranie i wypowiedźcie swoje zdanie teraz! Będzie to miało dla was bardzo duże znaczenie.

Głosowanie, jakie odbędzie się na tem zebraniu, będzie prowadzone podług starej metody amerykańskiej na zasadzie WIĘKSZOŚĆ DECYDUJE.

Przyjdźcie i powiedźcie co macie do powiedzenia, teraz! Potem będzie zapóźno!

 37

ORGANIZING EFFORTS utilized all possible approaches. Since the Polish community is one of Detroit's largest, handbills featured messages in its native tongue. Kelsey Hayes was one of the very first plants to be struck in Detroit. (Wayne)

126

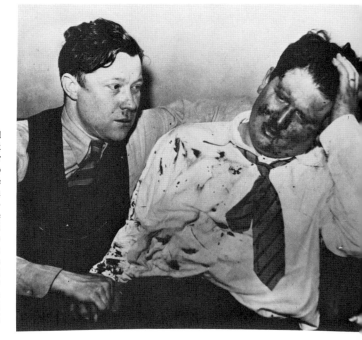

ONE BLOODY DAY *(left)* in May would produce what probably was the single most dramatic moment of the drive. Walter Reuther (at left) and Dick Frankensteen were in a group of UAW officials who went to the Ford Rouge plant on May 26, 1937, to participate as part of a large group of people intent on passing out hand-bills. As they walked across an overpass from the parking lot to the plant, a group of Ford employees approached them, and proceeded to beat them. The climax of that action came in April, 1941, when the UAW struck Ford and the company capitulated. UAW officials showed their delight as Harry Bennett *(below)* signed for Ford in June. To Bennett's right is Philip Murray, who was then president of the CIO, and to the left is UAW President R. J. Thomas, and Secretary George Addes. (Wayne)

ALL WAS NOT GRIM in the union drive of the 1930s and 1940s. This float, part of a Labor Day parade, helped to call attention to the Neisner clerks' drive. The result of all the activity was that Detroit turned from one of the most "open shop" cities in the country into one of its most strongly unionized. While the UAW played a dominant role, all segments—the Teamsters, Building Trades, and eventually municipal employees—gained strength. (Wayne)

CIVIL RIGHTS were on the minds of Detroiters early, as this group headed for the National Association for the Advancement of Colored People convention in Richmond, Virginia, in 1939 would testify. The Detroit NAACP chapter always has been among the largest in the country. (Wayne)

WHISTLE-STOPPING was big in 1936 when Franklin Roosevelt ran for his second term as President. His train drew a big crowd in Detroit. Right behind him is then-Governor of Michigan, Frank Murphy.

ONE OF DETROIT'S more colorful events over the years has been the unfurling on Flag Day of the world's largest flag on the front of the J. L. Hudson Building. The 90-by-123 foot banner, shown here as of June 1934, was first used on November 11, 1923. This patriotic gesture, the Thanksgiving Day parade in which Santa Claus makes his annual appearance, and later a fireworks display sponsored as part of the Freedom Festival, have been traditional J. L. Hudson contributions to the community. The store was founded in 1881 by Joseph L. Hudson and later was led by the Webber brothers and another J. L. Hudson who also played major roles in civic affairs. (News)

THE COMING OF THE CAR took some of the gleam off riding on the river, but in the 1930s and 1940s a day at Put-in-Bay, Tashmoo, or Bob Lo was still a big thing. (Burton)

A DAY AT THE MOVIES for Walter P. Chrysler in February 1936, found such stars on hand as Chester Morris, standing behind Mr. and Mrs. Chrysler (she's in the black coat), Clark Gable, and Melvyn Douglas, far right. (Chrysler)

REMEMBER THE J-HOP? This was 1936 and Wayne's class of '37 was having its big night out—the J-Hop which was the sort of tradition that faded after the War. This was the Grand March, highlight of the evening, at the Masonic Temple's Fountain Ballroom. (Wayne)

FOR DETROIT CATHOLICS there are no more poignant or meaningful moments than the departure of one bishop and the arrival of another. In 1937, the Most Rev. Edward Mooney *(above)*, who became a Cardinal in 1946, was met by Governor Frank Murphy and an honor guard of the Knights of Columbus *(below)*, when he arrived to replace Bishop Michael J. Gallagher, who had served the Diocese since November 18, 1918. Bishop Gallagher is shown *(left)* entering Holy Trinity Church on one occasion before his death on January 20, 1937. (Free Press)

OUT OF DETROIT came the Lone Ranger and the Green Hornet to add a touch of color to the radio fare of the late 1930s. Brace Beemer was the original man with a horse named Silver, and it was George W. Trendle who "created" everybody's hero at Station WXYZ. (Free Press)

IT WAS CHRISTMAS, and Frank Murphy who had been Mayor of Detroit, Governor of Michigan, Governor-General of the Philippines, and was to become a Supreme Court Justice, was home in 1939. At the moment he was the United States Attorney General in Franklin Roosevelt's cabinet. Mary Aurora Teahan, his niece, has her arm around his neck. At right are his sister Mrs. Marguerite Teahan and his two brothers, Harold Murphy and Recorder's Court Judge George Murphy. (Free Press)

133

COMMUNITY OF HOMES is what they call the Detroit area, and Joe Clark caught the mood of stability, of pride of ownership in this artistic photo of a street in Hamtramck. (HPL)

134

The Transitional 1940s

THE INCREDIBLE 30s were to be followed by the Transitional 40s.

First there was war, then an uneasy peace and finally a 250th birthday party. Even a city must relax, catch its breath, strive for new goals.

For Detroit, the first order of business was to serve as an "Arsenal of Democracy". Billions of dollars were spent here for the tanks, trucks, planes, and other materiel that helped to keep a huge military machine mobile.

It was done smoothly—but not without stresses.

A race riot gave the community its first deep insight into a problem that it would have to face up to for years to come. And then there was the post-war period of adjustment when a sudden demobilization brought with it equally sudden problems. There were shortages, inflation, strikes, and a surge that would bring Detroit to its peak population—almost 2 million in 1950.

Then there would come a time for rebuilding a city and revitalizing the spirit of the people.

ARMISTICE DAY, 1941, was more a preview of another war than a salute to a past peace. A few days after this parade there came the bombs at Pearl Harbor and then the mobilization of men and Detroit's machines for World War II. (Free Press)

THE HALLS at Wayne State University were filled with patriotic exhortations as students joined others in all-out support of World War II. (Wayne)

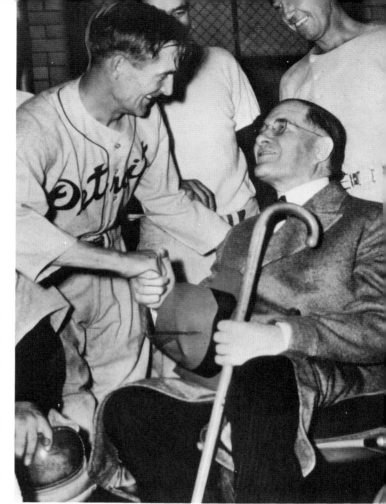

ONE FOR WALTER O. BRIGGS was the pennant won by the Detroit Tigers in 1940. Briggs had taken over from Frank Navin in 1936. He's shown congratulating Manager Del Baker in the lockerroom after the Tigers had clinched the pennant. They lost the World Series to Cincinnati in seven games. A couple of years later, First Baseman Hank Greenberg was a sergeant in the Army Air Corps but he came back in 1945, just in time to lead the Tigers to another pennant. He hit a four-run homer in the ninth inning of the last game of the season in St. Louis to beat the Browns, 6 to 3, and clinch it. That year the Tigers won the Series, beating Chicago, 4 games to 3. (Free Press)

HELP THE WHITE PEOPLE

To Keep This District WHITE

MEN NEEDED

TO KEEP OUR LINES SOLID

COME TO NEVADA and FENLON

Sunday and Monday

WE NEED HELP

Don't BE YELLOW COME OUT

We Need Every WHITE MAN

WE WANT OUR GIRLS TO WALK ON THE STREET NOT RAPED

OTHER RUMBLINGS were being heard on the home front where the first signs appeared of what was to become a great movement by black citizens for equality and justice at all levels. The first confrontation came in February 1942, when black families began to move into the Sojourner Truth project in the heavily Polish, all-white North Detroit area. Two attempts to block the influx of blacks were made before the moves could be completed, with thousands of troopers and police on hand. (Wayne)

PROTEST GROUPS were much more restrained in the 1940s. This one had gone to Washington from Detroit by train to protest the government's actions in handling the Sojourner Truth Housing project. After making its point with Senator Prentiss Brown, it posed at Urban League headquarters. (Wayne)

TENSION INCREASED in the months that followed until finally on June 20, 1943, a hot summer Sunday, trouble started on a jam-packed Belle Isle, spilled over the bridge onto Jefferson Avenue, and was fanned by rumors until it spread through the city. (Free Press)

U. S. TROOPS eventually had to be called in, and the toll wound up at 34 killed, 23 of them black, hundreds injured, 1,800 arrested, and property damage was in the millions. (Free Press)

A WILDLY CHEERING CROWD greeted V-J Day on August 15, 1945, in downtown Detroit, celebrating the end of World War II *(above)*. The Armistice Parade on November 15, 1945, was a little more subdued *(opposite page)* as the war was over—but our boys were still overseas, or at least many of them. The poster at lower left exhorts to "Invest in Victory—Bring the Boys Home." (Free Press)

DOMINANT POLITICAL figures in the 1940s in Detroit were Edward Jeffries, Jr. (standing), and Albert Cobo who started serving as treasurer in the late 1930s and gradually won favor for his fiscal policies. He was elected mayor himself in 1950. Jeffries was the first to begin to lay major plans for revitalizing Detroit—downtown and otherwise—but he had to sell his ideas at meetings such as this where a group of Detroit leaders was brought together to discuss the problem of blighted areas. (Free Press)

HENRY FORD I AND II share a moment together at an old lathe shortly after the transfer of the presidency of the company. Henry II became the boss on September 21, 1945, and proceeded to lead a major reorganization of the company. (Free Press)

ON THE DAY OF HIS LAST birthday, his 83rd, Henry and Mrs. Ford went to a birthday party at Ford Field, Dearborn, and were greeted by thousands, among them then 10-year-old Dick LeClair who presented Ford with a cake. Ford died on April 7, 1947. (Free Press)

11,000 BUTTONS from CIO locals made up this 54-pound costume worn by A. R. Beale during the Labor Day parade in 1947. Margaret Francis, of Local 742, is checking some of them. (Free Press)

TWO REUTHERS SHOT by would-be assassins were together with their brother Roy (center) during the 1949 UAW convention in Detroit. Victor (left) was recovering from a shotgun blast that had ripped into his face while he was sitting in his living room on May 24 that year. He eventually lost the sight of his right eye. Walter had been shot 13 months earlier while having a snack with his wife in their kitchen. His right arm was smashed. No one ever was convicted of either crime. (Free Press)

INTERNATIONAL flavor is provided by this lineup of costumed women *(below)* during a ball sponsored by the International Institute in 1949. It was a time when Detroit was becoming more and more conscious of its ethnic diversity. Emphasizing the point, one could also note that Polish dancers entertained at a garden party *(above)*, and that the Holy Family Church *(opposite page, top)*, a cherished landmark for the Italian community, was saved during an urban renewal spree. The church, founded in 1909, has been designated as the national church for Detroit's Italian Catholics. (Int. Institute)

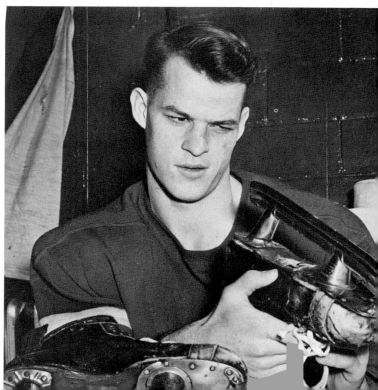

STARDOM CAME EARLY for Gordie
Howe who joined the Detroit Red Wings
for the 1946-47 season and quickly established himself as a high scorer. He came in
weighing 187 pounds, added about 10
more over the years, but always, as he did
from the start, focused on good condition-
ing exercises. (Free Press)

FOLLOWING TRADITION, Harry S. Truman came to Detroit on Labor Day in 1948 to kick off his "Give 'em Hell" campaign with a rally in Cadillac Square. The platform at old City Hall is filled on this day with leading Democrats, including Soapy Williams, the youngish looking fellow with the bow tie, who won his first term as governor in that November's election. (Detroit News)

OUT OF THE DETROIT area to run for governor in the late 1940s came G. Mennen Williams, with a bow tie and a penchant for dancing and personally meeting constituents. "Soapy" had the support of a handful of friends, including Jim and Kim Lincoln and Martha and Hicks Griffiths (Jim later became a judge and Martha a Congresswoman) when he launched his 1948 campaign. He surprised the pros by winning the primary and then trouncing Kim Sigler in the finals. It launched a new political era that would, in the long range, have significant meaning for Detroit. In this picture "Soapy" is shown dancing with Mrs. Elmer Erdig, a leader in the Hungarian community, at a local gathering. (Jellinek)

SHORTLIVED IS THE WORD for the automobile-building history of the Kaiser-Frazer corporation. It started after World War II when Henry Kaiser took over the former bomber plant at Willow Run. He began producing the small Henry J in 1947, was merged with Willys, and out of the passenger car field in the early 1950s. (Wayne)

SCANDINAVIAN
SYMPHONY ORCHEST
1940

A MAJOR AND VISIBLE expression of the role of the Scandinavians in Detroit's life was developed in the 1930s when scores of unemployed people, wanting to keep busy, got together to form the Scandinavian Symphony Orchestra. Their first concert was on February 18, 1931, and since then the orchestra has given several concerts a year, in addition to supporting several other choral and dancing groups. A feature is the

150

parading of the flags of all Scandinavian nations at the final concert of the year, such as on this occasion in 1940. Scandinavians have provided diverse contributions to Detroit and Michigan, ranging from the lumberjacks of the north to the skilled toolmakers of the auto industry. (McMullan)

A PICTURE OF RURAL America is this superb photograph by Joe Clark, one of Detroit's leading photographers. It features Henry Ford, whose interest in farming including production of tractors and ex-

periments with soybeans, was long standing. Ford stands next to an old steam threshing machine at a gathering in Tecumseh, Michigan, in the early 1940s. (HPL)

WITH THE WAR OVER, labor and management began wrestling again and a rash of strikes broke out. In this one, started at Chrysler May 12, 1948, the battle was over wages. It lasted 17 days and the UAW got a 13-cent-an-hour raise to $1.55 an hour. In 1950, the UAW struck Chrysler again, this time for 100 days, to win a company-paid and -funded pension plan. (Free Press)

ONE THING on which all Detroiters can agree is their desire to make the United Fund drive a success. This massive fund-raising effort for almost 200 agencies was started in 1949, with Walter Laidlaw running it, and has never failed to make its goal. A torchlighting ceremony has always kicked off the drive, and on this occasion, in October, 1950, W. Stuart Symington, then chairman of the National Security Resources Board, was on hand to do the honors in front of the old City Hall. (Free Press)

IF SOMEONE were to make an award to be given to the Detroiter most beloved for the longest period of time, it would go automatically to Edgar (Eddie) Guest whose poetry was a feature of the *Detroit Free Press* for decades and who became a national figure. Eddie was unstinting in his kindness and concern—and despite his acclaim always made it a point to insist that he was just another reporter for his newspaper. He started on the *Free Press* in 1895 as a summer fill-in, and stayed on the rest of his life. John Coppin was commissioned to paint his portrait. (Free Press)

FIRST JEWEL in the Civic Center crown is the Veterans Memorial Building which was dedicated on June 14, 1950. That year in a real way marks a milestone in the city's history. Urban renewal became the big thing in the months ahead, with great numbers of buildings being torn down and some new ones going up. The new beginnings for the second half of the 20th century, symbolically, may be marked by the picture of Mayor Albert Cobo *(facing page, center)* turning over the first spade of ground for the Douglass Housing project on the near East Side on May 6, 1950. Henry Durbin, housing commission chairman, shared the moment. A few months later, Cobo stood by as Mrs. Edsel Ford, with sons Benson and William Clay *(facing page, bottom)* opened the Edsel Ford Expressway to traffic. (Free Press)

IT WAS A HAPPY 250th birthday celebration highlighted by this cake-lighting ceremony in a fairyland setting in Grand Circus Park July 1951. Thousands gathered at the base of "the cake" at a moment when the Korean War was winding down—and a new era started for the United States and Detroit. (Free Press)

Preceding page: AN END AND A BEGINNING for Detroit. Standing out in bright, new splendor in the foreground is the Veterans Memorial Building, first of the Civic Center which was to develop through the 1950s and the 1960s. *Free Press* Chief Photographer Tony Spina took this aerial view which helps to point up in the 1970s—at a time when some despair—how far the city has come in still another rebuilding effort.

160